Living Faith

Living Faith

Lance Lambert

LANCE LAMBERT MINISTRIES

Richmond, Virginia, USA

ISBN: 978-1-68389-039-3

www.lancelambert.org

Contents

Preface

During June 1994 in Richmond, Virginia, Lance Lambert spoke four messages on Living Faith. The spoken word has been transcribed and edited into the four chapters contained in this book. The following excerpts touch upon the burden expressed through brother Lambert.

There is no more vital, strategic, necessary matter than living faith. We are living in days of artificiality and superficiality which is a very shallow kind of Christianity. It is a Christianity that is more on the surface—skin deep. We do not find today the depth of character, sacrifice, or endurance that once characterized the church of God. This is very largely because we are not the possessors of a living, working faith.

We need a living, working faith that links us to the Person of the Lord and brings us into all the reality of what He has so dearly won for us at Calvary.

The greatest need amongst us who love the Lord and are true believers is a genuine, living, working faith; there is no other faith.

Real faith is always alive; real faith is always working. There is no other faith. The faith that is in our head is nothing but human intelligence masquerading as Christianity. Real faith unites us to God. Real faith brings us into the will of God. Real faith brings us to the fruit of the Spirit. Real faith brings us into the anointing of the Holy Spirit. Real faith means that you and I are walking with the Lord in a contemporary manner.

1.
The Just Shall Live by Faith

Habakkuk 2:4

Behold, his soul is puffed up, it is not upright in him; but the righteous shall live by his faith.

Romans 1:16–17

For I am not ashamed of the gospel: for it is the power of God unto salvation to everyone that believeth; to the Jew first, and also to the Greek. For therein is revealed a righteousness of God from faith unto faith: as it is written, But the righteous shall live by faith.

Galatians 3:11

Now that no man is justified by the law before God, is evident: for, The righteous shall live by faith.

Hebrews 10:35–39

Cast not away therefore your boldness [confidence], which hath great recompense of reward. For ye have need of patience, that, having done the will of God, ye may receive the promise. For yet a very little while, He that cometh shall come,

and shall not tarry. But my *we are not of them that shrink*
righteous one shall live by faith: *back unto perdition; but of them*
And if he shrink back, my soul *that have faith unto the saving*
hath no pleasure in him. But *[gaining] of the soul.*

Shall we pray?

Beloved Lord, we want to thank You that we are gathered here in the name of our Messiah, the Lord Jesus; and we thank You, beloved Father, that You have made specific provision for us when we come to Your Word. We want to tell you, Lord, that apart from You we can do nothing. We can read, we can enunciate truth, we can hear many words; but unless You are here in the power and grace of this whole time, it will amount to nothing. Lord, we come by faith under that anointing for my speaking, for those who translate, and for all of us who hear. Let Your design and purpose in our time be fulfilled, oh Lord, and we shall give You all the praise and all the glory. In the name of our Lord Jesus. Amen.

Our Lord Jesus told a quite remarkable story about a judge who was corrupt (see Luke 18:1–8). There are corrupt judges. Sadly, this is probably true of the United States, as it is certainly true of every part of Asia, from the Far East to west Asia, where I live. The judge in this story took gifts on the side. He deferred judgment; he would not in any way give judgment until the gift was commensurate with the judgment that he felt the person wanted to have.

In this story that Jesus told there was a little widow. She had no money, she had no influence, she had no prestige, and she had no status. She had the only thing most widows have, and that was a tongue. Being Jewish, she used her tongue to the fullest extent. She went again and again to that judge. In our English version, it says, "I must do something about this lest she wear me out." But a very interesting word is used in the Greek; it says, "I must do something about this lest she bruise me." With her tongue, she battered that judge until, finally, in desperation he decided that he had to do something. So he asked her what she wanted. That is the most remarkable thing! She said, "This and this and this." He said, "You have it; now go and do not trouble me anymore." Whether he put it in writing, I do not know, but that is the end of the story.

Then our Lord said, "If this was true of such a corrupt judge, how much more is it true of the righteous Judge;" that is, our Father in heaven. Then He went on to say that He will avenge the blood of His elect. He said, "Nevertheless, shall the Son of man find faith on the earth when he cometh?" It has been understood by some that this means that there will be no salvation, no living faith, no one who can exercise faith at the very last phase of world history. I do not accept that because the prophet Joel, speaking of the days in which we live and of the very last days of world history, when there will be signs in the sun and moon and stars and pillars of smoke on the earth, said, "And whosoever shall call on the name of the Lord shall be saved." So it is my conviction that right up to the very end, the Lord will continue to save those who come to Him through faith.

Then what did our Lord mean in telling this story? This is quite an extraordinary story, a very vivid story. Why did He tell it unless He was saying, "When the Son of man comes, will He find overcoming faith on the earth? Will He find enduring faith on the earth? Will He find persevering faith on this earth?" I want you to note that He asked a question; He did not make a statement. He did not say that when the Son of man comes, He will not find such faith on the earth. He said, "And when the Son of man comes, shall He find faith such as this woman had on this earth?"

It is very important that we should understand that the apostle Paul, speaking of these very days in which we live, said, "But we should put on the breastplate of faith and love, and for a helmet, the hope of salvation" (see 1 Thessalonians 5:8). In other words, however dark things get, however much the current flows against us, we are those who can experience, who can know, who can possess a living, working, practical faith right up to the coming of the Lord.

Worldwide Unbelief

We are living in days of unbelief. We are living in days of cynicism. We are living, I suppose it would be correct to say, in a neo-pagan society. It has been called the post-Christian society. It certainly is neo-paganism that is influencing every level of society. You know the battle the United States is in. You know the forces of cynical unbelief that are mounting every weapon that can be mobilized in order to destroy any Biblical principles that might still be operative in the society of this nation. But it is the same all over the world; it is a world-wide phenomenon.

This cynicism, this unbelief, this neo-paganism that is influencing our whole attitude and our concepts to every-thing—life, behavior, education, medicine, research—is also influencing the believers. This spirit of cynicism, this spirit of unbelief, in many ways, is influencing those who really know the Lord. So we find within Christian circles, just under the surface, a cynicism, a Christian cynicism: "Apparently, the Lord was able to work miracles thousands of years ago, but He does not do it any more."

I am so much concerned and grieved by those who stand against any form of miracles in our day, as if it all went out with the canon of the New Testament. If it was an honestly held view, I would respect it; but in the majority of cases I have known, it is cynicism. Such people have never experienced a miracle in their lives. Therefore, their attitude is that there is no such thing as a miracle in our day. But if you and I are born of God, that is the greatest miracle of all. If God can save an unsaved sinner, a sinner without hope; if He can justify that sinner, unite him to Himself in the Lord Jesus, and change him into the likeness of the Lord Jesus—if that is not a miracle, what is? Once we admit to a miracle such as that—the miracle of the indwelling of the Lord Jesus, the miracle of His speaking to us, the miracle of Him revealing Himself to us—then we have admitted everything. There is nothing that is impossible; there is nothing the Lord cannot do. But this cynicism, this terrible, intelligent, academic, seemly sophisticated cynicism that lies just beneath the surface of so many believers, so many assemblies and fellowships, is an evil heart of unbelief—nothing less and nothing more. It alienates us from the work of the Holy Spirit. It divorces us from the work of the Lord Jesus. It somehow distances us from everything the Lord wants to do in involving us in the fulfillment of His purpose. Therefore, I believe that this matter of faith is vital. Of course, it is linked with revelation and with experience.

Living on the Principle of Faith

The greatest need amongst us who love the Lord and are true believers is a genuine, living, working faith; there is no other faith. Real faith is always alive; real faith is always working. There is no other faith. The faith that is in our head is nothing but human intelligence masquerading as Christianity. Real faith unites us to God. Real faith brings us into the will of God. Real faith brings us to the fruit of the Spirit. Real faith brings us into the anointing of the Holy Spirit. Real faith means that you and I are walking with the Lord in a contemporary manner.

Four times in the word of God this little phrase is found (quoting the King James version): "The just shall live by faith." It is in Habakkuk 2:4, Romans 1:17, Galatians 3:11, and Hebrews 10:38. When anything is repeated in the Word of God, it is fundamental, and its significance can never be exaggerated. I believe that alone means that you and I need to wake up. The greatest need for those who have been born into Christian homes is to experience a living, practical, working faith. There is no need to be a second generation, living on your parent's faith, but you need to know for yourself a faith that is the gift of God that unites you in an original way to the Lord.

Notice that the Lord first said this to Habakkuk. Now Habakkuk was a very interesting man. He lived in days very much like our own. He was waiting for judgment. He was waiting for the fulfillment of the Word of God concerning the judgment of his nation and the judgment of nations around him. Everything seemed so dark. Nobody listened. It was a day of decline, a day of unbelief, a day of contradiction, a day when people were no longer faithful to the Lord, and in it the Lord said that He had no pleasure in him who was not straight inside and whose soul was puffed up. Then He said, "But the righteous shall live by his faith." That is the first thing I want you to notice. However dark it may be, whatever judgments may be coming upon the world, however much we may have to face in this very difficult period of tremendous change and the fulfillment of so much that is predicted in the word of God, we have this marvelous word: "The just, the righteous shall live by his faith."

We have this word in Romans, right at the beginning of this greatest exposition in the Bible of the gospel of the good news. Paul said, "For I am not ashamed of the gospel: for it is the power of God unto salvation to everyone that believeth; to the Jew first, and also to the Greek. For therein is revealed a righteousness of God from faith unto faith: as it is written, But the righteous [just] shall live by faith" (Romans 1:16–17).

Notice the words shall live. The Lord could just as easily have said, "The just shall be saved by faith;" but He did not say that. Not that it is not true, because the just are saved through faith; but to live is something more. It is not just an initial experience of salvation, but the righteous, the one who is justified by the grace of God shall live by faith. In other words, death and corruption come into our experience through unbelief; but faith comes through life. We live by faith.

The translation of J.N. Darby puts it like this: "The righteous or just shall live on the principle of faith." In the Hebrew, it says that the righteous shall live by his faith, meaning that it is not just an initial thing. It is something that underlies the whole living of the righteous, of the faithful, of the true believer. In the Greek, the word is from: "The just shall live from his faith." So J.N. Darby quite correctly translated it, adding a word that is not there in the original: "The just shall live on the principle of faith"—which is exactly right. We have come right to the heart of the matter. If you want to live the Christian life, if you want to live in the fullness of God, if you want to live in the grace of God, in the power of God, if you want to live in the possibility of being changed into the likeness of His Son, then you have to live on the principle of faith. We were saved on the principle of faith, we were justified on the principle of faith, but every fresh step forward into experiencing the Lord has to be on the principle of faith. If by the grace of God the work of the Lord is completed in our lives, perfected in our lives, it will be on the principle of faith. God has never operated on any other principle.

At the very beginning, when Abel offered a lamb and Cain offered the fruit of his toil, Cain was rejected and Abel was accepted. People think that was very mean and severe of the Lord. After all, Cain was a husbandman, a market gardener, and he only brought the fruit of his toil. Whereas Abel was a shepherd which was his business, so he brought a lamb. It would have been strange if Abel had decided to bring fruit to offer to the Lord. Both of them brought the toil of their work; the Lord accepted the one and rejected the other. I believe there was much more to it than that.

When the Lord covered Adam and Eve, He covered them with skins, and according to our tradition, it was a lamb. Somehow, it was passed on to Adam and Eve and their children that only through the blood of a lamb could one find salvation. Cain very easily could have asked his brother for a lamb, but there must have been some bad feeling between those brothers; otherwise, he would never have murdered his brother. If there was bad feeling, such as jealousy or rivalry, he would not have gone to his brother and asked for one of his lambs so that he could be accepted by God. I have no doubt at all that Cain knew very well that the only way to be accepted was by the blood of a lamb. That was the principle of faith.

All the way through the Word, whether it was Noah or Abraham, whether it was Jacob or Joseph, whether it was Moses or Joshua, we find the same thing: they lived on the principle of faith. Everything is on this principle.

In Romans 1:17a, it says, "For therein is revealed a righteousness of God from faith unto faith," as if every-thing is from faith. Have you been gifted with the gift of faith? Have you been saved by the grace of God through faith? That is faith. There is the foundation. But every further step in a discovery of your so great salvation, every new, deeper appropriation of what is yours in the work of the Lord Jesus on the cross and made available to you through the Holy Spirit, every single fresh step forward is from faith to faith. No matter how old we get, no matter how much knowledge we accumulate, no matter how much experience we might have, at the very end it will still be faith. It is from faith to faith.

Self-Manufactured Christianity

I would like to make two further statements from the Word of God, both of which are stark in their solemnity and unbelievably challenging. It sums up this whole thing. The first is in Romans 14:23b: "Whatsoever is not of faith is sin." That seems like a horribly stark word. "Whatsoever is not of faith"—that is, through faith, from faith—"is sin." It is not just negative thought or just some difficulty on our part. If it is not through faith, then it belongs to the realm of sin—to fallen man, to the first man, to Adam—to everything that comes out of him. It is sin. That is a very severe word. So much of my Christianity and your Christianity is self-manufactured. It is a question of culture or maybe it is a natural inheritance. Sometimes it comes through academic pursuit. Because some of us are more intelligent than others, we are more easily able to manipulate the Word of God. It is a terrible thing to say: "Whatsoever is not of faith is sin." That means you can study the Bible with your brain, without living faith, and it is all sin. That means you can be christened or baptized or sign a thousand decision cards, and if it is not a real work of the Lord through faith, it is sin. It means that you and I can join the church and if we have not had a saving experience of the Lord Jesus, it is sin. It is a very stark word. It is an epitaph written on all self manufactured Christianity. "Whatsoever is not of faith is sin."

Without Faith We Cannot Please God

Here is the second word. It is a little more comforting, but only a little more. In Hebrews 11:6, it says, "Without faith it is impossible to please God." In some of the modern versions, it says, "It is impossible to be well-pleasing to Him." The Word of God says quite clearly that if there is no faith, no matter what you do, you cannot please the Lord. Without faith it is impossible to please the Lord; it is impossible to get the "Well done, good and faithful servant;" it is impossible to be well-pleasing to Him. So we are at the heart of the whole thing.

Saved Through Faith

We have looked at this little statement, "The just shall live by faith," and then we have added these two very stark statements to it. Now we can see what comes to us through faith. First, we are saved through faith. In Ephesians 2:8–9, it says, "For by grace have ye been saved through faith; and that not of yourselves, it is the gift of God; not of works, that no man should glory [boast]." No man should glory in this thing; it is the gift of God. It is by grace ye are saved through faith; and that not of yourselves, it is the gift of God. Faith is not a natural thing, it is not something you stir up from within you, it is not something you can somehow or other gather together from within your own being; it is the gift of God. So by grace are you saved through faith, and even the faith through which you are saved by the grace of God is God-given. Therefore, you have absolutely no ground whatsoever to boast—that it was your pedigree or your background or your national background or your racial background. Whatever it is, you have no ground whatsoever to boast in any shape or form, for you have been saved by the grace of God through faith;

and that faith is not of yourselves, it is God's gift; it is not of works, that no man should glory.

Justified Through Faith

The second thing is that we are justified. How wonderful this is! "Being therefore justified by faith, we have peace with God through our Lord Jesus Christ; through whom also we have had our access by faith into this grace wherein we stand" (Romans 5:1–2a). How rarely we hear about justification in the assemblies of God's people. Yet justification is one of the most tremendous doctrines in the word of God. We are justified through the finished work of our Lord Jesus. That means you have been declared righteous by none other than God Himself. On the basis that the Lord Jesus, who knew no sin, became your sin, God has declared that you are His righteousness in Christ. It is so amazing!

So many Christians suffer from bad consciences, from guilt, from things they have done in the past. The enemy has marvelous ground to work on us with, and we do not know how to stand before those accusations of the powers of darkness and evil. But it is through the shield of faith that we can parry every fiery dart of the evil one. Who really knows the wonder of justification? To whom has it been revealed that they are justified by the Lord Jesus and His work? Through faith we are justified.

Standing by Faith

"By their unbelief they were broken off, and thou standest by thy faith" (Romans 11:20a). We stand by faith. We do not go forward;

we do not go backward; we stand. As it says in Ephesians 6, we stand and withstand and having done all we stand. Then we know the victory of the Lord. It is by faith we stand. The first thing is we are saved by faith, we are justified by faith, and we stand by faith. We are not knocked over nor driven back through the battle; but we stand by faith.

Walking by Faith

"For we walk by faith, not by sight" (II Corinthians 5:7). Now we are walking. When we walk, we take a whole series of steps; it is step after step. How else do we walk? We are so used to walking that nobody thinks about it. We do not read a book about walking. It is only when we get a gamy leg or break a leg or sprain an ankle that we suddenly realize what an amazing thing it is to walk without any problem. You never think about walking, do you? You just take a whole series of steps. If I want to get out of here, I have to walk; that is the only way out. I take one step after the other and in a few moments I am out.

We walk by faith, that is, we take step after step by faith. The first step we ever took was by faith, the second step we ever took was by faith, the third step we ever took was by faith; and that is how we progress. As we move on, we walk by faith. Some people get all tied up on this kind of thing. They need such a lot to take one step of faith. It is such a natural, spiritually-natural, normal thing to walk; and we walk by faith. So when the Lord is dealing with you, let Him. By faith, take the step, and you have taken another step forward. So you walk by faith.

Running the Race

Then we run. This is something more. What is running? It is only walking in a much quicker manner. "Therefore let us also, seeing we are compassed about with so great a cloud of witnesses, lay aside every weight, and the sin which doth so easily beset us, and let us run with patience the race that is set before us, looking unto Jesus the author and perfecter of our faith" (Hebrews 12:1-2a). We run by faith. It is not just that we are progressing in a very quick and fast manner. That is not the idea. The idea in this race is that it has a goal; it has an objective; there is a course. We do not just run anywhere; we are running in a race. It is a set course, and we are not going to be diverted; we are going to run right through. Jesus is the initiator, and through Him we start the race, and by Him we finish the race. There is no other way. It is by faith.

The Fight of Faith

"Fight the good fight of the faith, lay hold on the life eternal, whereunto thou wast called" (1 Timothy 6:12a). Fight the good fight of faith. Now we discover there is a battle, there is a conflict. This is not something that has no enemy in it. We have an enemy and we have to fight the good fight of faith; we have to lay hold on life eternal. Because this is the fight of faith, if there is an evil heart of unbelief, the enemy will come in and knock you out from the beginning. At some point, if not from the beginning, you will be knocked out. We have to learn that it is the fight of faith.

Inheriting Through Faith

Lastly, in this matter, there is inheriting. "That ye be not sluggish, but imitators of them who through faith and patience inherit the promises" (Hebrews 6:12). We discover that we inherit the promises through faith and patience. It is not just through faith, but also patience. It is enduring faith, faith that persists, faith that perseveres; it is overcoming faith.

The whole gamut of the Christian life, of Christian service, of the fellowship of the church is to do with faith. It begins with faith, it perseveres through faith, it is built up and developed through faith, and it is completed through faith.

Living Faith Puts You in Christ Jesus

Now I want to look at this little phrase "Believe on the Lord Jesus Christ." When the Lord first showed this to me, it revolutionized my whole attitude on this question. Have you ever asked yourself why we have that strange little phrase "Believe on the Lord Jesus Christ and thou shall be saved"? You do not believe on people, do you? You believe in people. You either believe in a person or you do not believe in a person. What is believing on a person? Why does the Bible speak about believing on? "For God so loved the world, that he gave his only begotten Son, that whosoever believeth on him should not perish, but have eternal life" (John 3:16). This is everywhere in the New Testament, particularly in John's gospels and letters. We have it again in John 3:36: "He that believeth on the Son hath eternal life."

When the old, godly translators of the King James Version came to this Greek phrase, they just did not know how to put it in English. They felt that if they said, "For God so loved the world, that He gave His only begotten Son, that whosoever believeth in Him should not perish, but have everlasting life," it just would not convey the meaning of the original. They felt the meaning of the word was very, very important; it was vital. So they coined a new phrase in English: "For God so loved the world, that He gave His only begotten Son, that whosoever believeth on Him should not perish." Actually, the word is literally: "For God so loved the world, that He gave His only begotten Son, that whosoever believeth into Him should not perish, but have everlasting life." Everywhere you go in the New Testament, wherever you have that little phrase "Believe on the Lord Jesus," it is actually, literally "Believe into the Lord Jesus." In other words, living faith takes you, moves you, mobilizes you; it is not static. It is not that somehow you stay here and remain yourself and He remains Himself and you believe in Him over there with some kind of mental assent, some kind of academic faith or belief. No; this living, working faith means you leave the position on which you were born, the foundation upon which you have thus far lived an unsaved life and you move by the grace of God into Christ. When God saves you, He puts you in the Lord Jesus. You are in Christ. Now do you understand why the Lord Jesus said, "Abide in Me and I in you"? That is where God has put you through living faith.

"By grace have you been saved through faith." When that faith was given to you, as far as God was concerned, your whole position and status changed. You were delivered from the power of darkness and transferred into the kingdom of God's dear Son.

In other words, whether you know it or not, a deliverance took place. The chains that had bound you to the powers of darkness, to an old life, to a fallen mankind were snapped and you were transferred into the kingdom of God's dear Son. Does that mean anything to you? The simplest person who has believed on the Lord Jesus has believed into Christ. It is living faith. You could not get into Him yourself. There was no way that you could change your position; you could not do it. No matter if you wept for years, no matter if you went to a thousand theological seminaries, no matter if you had so many theological degrees after your name that the whole alphabet was exhausted, it would not matter for one single moment. It would not do anything to you at all. No matter how many good works you did, what penances you made, how penitent you seemed, it would not in any way change your position. You were unable to do it. God did it in the moment that you believed. That is living faith.

The Unspeakable Gift of God

God has not given us a thing called salvation. He has not even given us an experience called salvation. He has given us a Person. That Person is the Lord Jesus. A child of God who does not know the Lord is a contradiction in terms. Yet, there are many believers who do not know the Lord. They have been saved but they are stuck there; they have not gone beyond. It is very, very sad. God has not given us all kinds of experiences like salvation, peace, joy, fulness, power; they are all gifts. God has given us a Person, and He has made that Person salvation. The name of Jesus in Hebrew is Yeshua; it means salvation. The Lord is salvation—

Yeshua. God makes the Lord Jesus joy in you. He makes Him peace in you. It is the peace of God, the peace which passes understanding. God makes the Lord Jesus life: "I am the life." God makes the Lord Jesus reality to you: "I am the truth." God makes the Lord Jesus the way ahead: "I am the way." God makes the Lord Jesus resurrection when you are dead. God makes the Lord Jesus everything you need. All the treasures of wisdom and knowledge are in Him; all the fulness of God is in Him; all the life of God is in Him. God has not given us things; He has given us a Person. That is why the apostle Paul said, "Thanks be to God for His unspeakable gift." That is why the apostle Paul said, "That I may know Him." In the Greek, there is a little suffix: "That I may fully know Him." Knowing about a person is altogether different from knowing a person.

I am always thankful that as rotten as I am and as full of weakness and failings as I am, that from the very beginning of my little Christian life, I understood that I had to know the Lord—not things, not experiences, but a Person. And as I got to know Him, everything would be explained and I would discover that I was overcoming when I least expected it, simply by knowing Him, simply by getting to know Him, simply by experiencing Him.

The Language of God

In the last book of the Bible, the Lord Jesus says, "I am the Alpha and Omega, the first and the last, the beginning and the end" (Revelation 22:13). What did He mean? Alpha is the first letter of the Greek alphabet and Omega is the last letter. What I would say is A and Zed, and you would say A and Z. What did the

Lord Jesus mean when He said, "I am A and Zed"? Did He mean that He is only the first and last letters and all the other letters are something else? Of course not! The Lord Jesus was saying, "I am the alphabet. I am the very language of God. When God speaks, I am His language." Do you want to understand the mind of God? Do you want to understand the heart of God? You have to understand it through the Lord Jesus. "I am Alpha and Omega." Outside of the Lord Jesus, there is no heavenly language; there is no language of God. He is God's language. He is the beginning and the end. Does that mean He is only the beginning and the end and everything in between is doing the best we can? No; it means He is everything. What does not originate with Him will never end with Him. But sadly, you can start with Him and not end with Him. Whether it is the church of God or whether it is the individual believer, Jesus is the beginning and the end and everything in between.

The Christian life is nothing other than the Lord Jesus by the Holy Spirit living His life in you and me. It is so simple, but we make it so complex, so difficult. People are always coming to me, especially young people, and asking me to explain the Christian life to them: "How can I live the Christian life?" I always say to them that the answer to living the Christian life is very simple; it is Jesus. They say, "How do I live Jesus?" I say to them: "That is an even simpler answer. The problem is not how to live; the problem is how to die. If you will die you will know the life."

In the last book of the Bible, He summed up everything in the statement He made in Revelation 22:13 in which He said that everything that is not in Him will not come through. You will never find anything that is not of the Lord Jesus in the city of God;

it is all out of Him. So you begin to understand that the righteous, the justified, the just shall live on the principle of faith.

Man is rendered absolutely helpless before God. No matter what his gifts are—whether it be his talents, his energy, his zeal, how religious he is, how intelligent he is, what knowledge he has—none of it brings him into the life of God. Man can be a genius in himself, but when it comes to God, he is helpless. He will get absolutely nowhere. That is why in the prophecy of Isaiah, it says, "I only am God. I only am the Savior" (see Isaiah 43:11, 45:21–22). There is no other Savior besides God; and there is no way to be saved or to enter into the life of God and all the fulness of God except through faith, and that is the gift of God.

Living Faith Connects You to God

I know that this will raise all kinds of questions for you. You will say, "Oh, if only I had more faith"; but you do not need more faith. Some of you have waited twenty years for more faith. You will not get it; you will die waiting for more faith. Then people say, "But it is Biblical to say, 'Lord increase our faith.'" The Lord said, "If you had faith as a grain of mustard seed, you would say to this sycamine tree (which is one of the biggest trees in our part of the world), 'Be removed, and be planted in the sea'" (see Luke 17:6). People think that is funny—to see a tree like that planted in the sea. Do not say the Lord does not have humor. "Be thou removed and planted in the sea"—and it shall be planted in the sea. Now the Lord did not mean: "Come on, you must have faith and you can move trees into the sea." That is not what He was saying. They had said, "Lord, increase our faith;" and He was saying,

"You do not need more faith. What you need is to use the little faith that you have. If you would only use that little faith by which you have been saved by the grace of God, if you would only live on the principle of that faith, then nothing would be impossible to you."

May the Lord help us. We are going to move into days when there will be less and less faith and more and more facade. There is going to be more and more of what we would call Hollywood style Christianity and less and less of the real article. The key to knowing the Lord is living faith. May God challenge us and wake us up, if necessary, that we at least might know that we are hopeless and helpless in ourselves. Then maybe He can shine into our hearts with an understanding of the way that faith operates. Faith is not something that you somehow or other engineer yourself and sort of gather up every last drop of it within you and push it together in one final push to see something happen in your life. That is not the way of faith. That is what I call Christian Science faith. You believe that something is not there and if you say it enough, it won't be. It is mind over matter, and that is something inside of man. It is not unknown to Buddhism; it is not unknown to Hinduism; it is not unknown to the most mystical form of Islam. This kind of faith is man's faith. If it is mind over matter, it is psychology; it is not faith. It is not Biblical faith; it is not genuine faith.

The faith that is the gift of God is something so small that you can overlook it; but when it operates, it connects you to the almighty infinity of God. When you are introduced into the fathomless fulness of God, nothing is impossible; nothing. Everything that God ever wanted in your life can be fulfilled.

It is possible. It is faith that is so small that we overlook it; but that kind of faith connects you to the power of God, to the grace of God, to the life of God, and to the fulness of God. May He open the eyes of our hearts.

Shall we pray?

Beloved Lord, there is not one of us that is not in need of living, working faith. We need to be delivered from all that is self-manufactured, all that is dead, academic faith. We need to be delivered from it, Lord. We need a faith that works, a faith that unites us to Your word, a faith that unites us to Your purpose, a faith that brings us in a new way into Your heart, a faith that somehow or other triumphs in darkness and in suffering, a faith that cries, "It shall be done." Oh Lord, we need that kind of faith. Open our eyes. Open the eyes of our hearts. Fill us with a new vision of Yourself, Lord. Somehow, link the smallness and finiteness of all of us to Your infinity. We ask it in the name of our Lord Jesus. Amen.

2.
The Power of Living Faith

Matthew 17:20

And [Jesus] saith unto them, Because of your little faith: for verily I say unto you, If ye have faith as a grain of mustard seed, ye shall say unto this mountain, Remove hence to yonder place; and it shall remove; and nothing shall be impossible unto you.

Luke 17:5–6

And the apostles said unto the Lord, Increase our faith. And the Lord said, If ye had faith as a grain of mustard seed, ye would say unto this sycamine tree, Be thou rooted up, and be thou planted in the sea; and it would obey you.

Matthew 8:23–27

And when [Jesus] was entered into a boat, his disciples followed him. And behold, there arose a great tempest in the sea, insomuch that the boat was covered with the waves: but he was asleep. And they came to him, and awoke him, saying, Save Lord; we perish. And he saith unto them, why are ye fearful, O ye of little faith?

Then he arose, and rebuked the winds and the sea; and there was a great calm. And the men marvelled, saying, What manner of man is this, that even the winds and the sea obey him?

Matthew 14:22–33

And straightway [Jesus] constrained the disciples to enter into the boat, and to go before him unto the other side, till he should send the multitudes away. And after he had sent the multitudes away, he went up into the mountain apart to pray: and when even was come, he was there alone. But the boat was now in the midst of the sea, distressed by the waves; for the wind was contrary. And in the fourth watch of the night he came unto them, walking upon the sea. And when the disciples saw him walking on the sea, they were troubled, saying, It is a ghost; and they cried out for fear. But straightway Jesus spake unto them, saying, Be of good cheer; it is I; be not afraid. And Peter answered him and said, Lord, if it be thou, bid me come unto thee upon the waters. And he said, Come. And Peter went down from the boat, and walked upon the waters to come to Jesus. But when he saw the wind, he was afraid; and beginning to sink, he cried out, saying, Lord, save me. And immediately Jesus stretched forth his hand, and took hold of him, and saith unto him, O thou of little faith, wherefore didst thou doubt? And when they were gone up into the boat, the wind ceased. And they that were in the boat worshipped him, saying, Of a truth thou art the Son of God.

Shall we pray?

Dear beloved Lord, we do want to thank You that we are gathered here in Your presence and in the name of our Lord Jesus. Father, together, we want to tell You we need You, and we praise You that You are always ready to meet need when we confess it. We need Your anointing on speaking, on any translation there may be, and upon our hearing. We do not want this time to be wasted time, not even just the outline of truths, fundamental and important as they may be. We want You to take this time and meet with us. To that end, by faith, we come under that anointing that You have provided that my speaking may be absolutely by Your enabling and our hearing may be Your enabling, so that Your purpose in our time may be fulfilled and something would be done in our lives that will never be taken away. Lord, hear us. We commit ourselves to You with thanksgiving and praise in the name of our Lord Jesus. Amen.

There is a tremendous need of living, working faith because we are living in a neo-pagan society. We are living in a society which basically has renounced Biblical principles. We are living in a society which is forsaking the revealed law of God, and in its place there has come in everything that comes out of man. The cynicism and unbelief are influencing believers everywhere. Especially in those countries that have seen the greatest work of the Holy Spirit in centuries gone by, we now discover the most terrible works of darkness. This cynicism and this spirit of unbelief is influencing true believers. That is why no amount of mental assent or academic recognition of truth is enough.

We need a genuine, living, working faith. That is the only answer in these last days into which we have entered.

The normal fallacy that we find amongst Christians concerning this matter of faith is that faith is power. There could be nothing further from the truth. It sounds like this: the greater faith you have, the greater power you will have. In other words, the greater the faith, the greater the power. It is not true; it is a fallacy. Actually, there is no power in faith. Power belongs to the Lord; power is in the Lord. Faith is what connects you to the power of God. Faith is what introduces you into the life of God, the wisdom of God, the power of God, and the fulness of God.

Seeing the Greatness of the Lord

When the apostle Paul was speaking to the church in Corinth, he used this little phrase: "That your faith should not stand in the wisdom of men, but in the power of God" (1 Corinthians 2:5). It is faith standing in the power of God. Faith in itself is not power. It does not have attributes in itself. Faith is merely that which brings us into the power of God, the reality of God's Word, the fulfillment of His purpose, and a living walk with Him. That is why faith is so vital, so strategic, so important. How can we explain faith? It is the link or the thing that brings us into a living relationship with God.

Our fellowships or our assemblies are filled with people who believe, but nothing ever happens. I used to be amused when I read the New Testament and came across that little phrase: "The demons believe and tremble." It is a good deal more than some believers. They are so used to the Word of God. They believe it from cover to cover—from Genesis to Revelation. They are absolutely convinced that it is authoritative, inspired, relevant, wholly accurate; but there is no experience of it. It has not become flesh and blood. It has not been translated into experience. Faith is the link. Once we begin to see this, it changes our whole mentality, and we begin to put the emphasis in the right place. Instead of putting the emphasis on faith, we begin to put it on the Lord. It is not our great faith that counts; it is our great Lord. Once you begin to see the greatness of the Lord, once you begin to understand the reality of His power and fullness, then faith is created in you that links you to it.

Consider our Lord's words in Matthew 17. There was a demonized lad and the disciples could not understand why they could not do anything about it. Apparently they prayed, speaking the correct formula over him, but nothing happened. Finally, they came to the Lord and said, "Why could we not do anything?" The Lord said, "Because of your little faith." Now thus far, this falls absolutely in line with the normal Christian's idea: "That is right, absolutely right, Lord. It is our little faith. We need more faith. We could not touch this demonic situation because of our little faith; we need more."

Upon this, the enemy comes in with his whole propaganda machine and says, "Absolutely right. You have hit the nail on the head; you need more faith. You go to all the conferences and take notes and wait until you get more faith. When you have greater faith, something will happen in your circumstances, something will happen in your life, something will happen in your family, something will happen amongst your business colleagues. But you have got to wait until the Lord gives you greater faith."

Some of us spend our whole lives waiting for more faith. We go through year after year after year after year waiting for greater faith, waiting for our faith to increase. We study ourselves, as it were, and look at the condition of our faith: Is it more this year or less? The more we look at it, the smaller it becomes; it shrinks, almost visibly, before our eyes. Once we become self-conscious about faith, it disappears. The little faith we once had, which worked and somehow functioned, disappears as we investigate it. We look at it under a microscope or through a magnifying glass, and then we say, "Oh, how little faith I have! I wish I was like some of those great saints that were credulous, perhaps superstitious. Maybe it helps to be like that."

Some think the normal way is that if you are intelligent, you cannot have a living, working faith; but if you come from a totally uneducated, unintelligent background and your intelligence is minimal, thank God, you will be a person who is a candidate for faith. You are going to have a faith that works because you are credulous. You are the kind of person who does not set sail on Friday, the 13th, or walk under a ladder, and because of this simple kind of attitude and believe anything once you get saved, you are a candidate for faith. It comes natural to people who are simple.

Now of course, none of us will say stupid; we say simple. But in Christian circles, when you speak of someone as simple, it is hardly ever a compliment. It is that amazing way that Christians have of stabbing someone. We say, "I wish I was simple like so and so, but I have intelligence. It is a great shame I was blessed with this intelligence and am rather academic. As a result, I find faith very difficult. I wish I was like so and so who is so simple." Actually, that is not what we really think. We think, "So and so is dumb and stupid and credulous and superstitious, and therefore can believe. But I am sophisticated, educated, intelligent, and I have a very hard time believing."

When the Lord said, "Because of your little faith," we immediately understand. "Yes, that is right; we need more faith. We need our faith to be increased because now we are in a trap." We read a book, we go to a conference, we get into some little circle of believers in order that our faith may be increased. Twenty years later we are still waiting; thirty years later we are still waiting. Faith has not increased, and nothing has happened.

It is like the children of Israel in the wilderness who circled round and round and round and round but got nowhere. The things of God were there, the miracles of God were there, the Word of God was there, the pillar of cloud and fire were there; everything was there, but they were not getting anywhere.

We are going round and round. We are waiting for something to happen: "My faith will suddenly burst out of its littleness into greatness; then I will be changed into His likeness, then I will know the crucified life, then I shall know the indwelling of the Lord in fullness, then I shall know the anointing of the Holy Spirit. But until then, I have to wait for my faith to be increased."

Faith as a Grain of Mustard Seed

Our Lord went on to explain what He meant. He said, "Because of your little faith: for verily I say unto you, If ye have faith as a grain of mustard seed, ye shall say unto this mountain,

Remove hence to yonder place; and it shall remove; and nothing shall be impossible unto you" (Matthew 17:20).

It is the same thing in Luke. "The apostles came to the Lord and said, Increase our faith. And the Lord said, If ye had faith as a grain of mustard seed, ye would say unto this sycamine tree (which is one of the largest trees in the Promised Land), Be thou rooted up, and be thou planted in the sea; and it would obey you" (Luke 17:5–6).

"Faith as a grain of mustard seed." Have you seen a mustard seed? If I had a handful of mustard seed in the palm of my hand, it could not be seen very well from a short distance away. But if I took one grain of mustard seed and put it in the palm of my hand, it would be very difficult to see it unless you were close to me and had good sight. Our Lord said that is all you need to remove a mountain. Now obviously, our Lord did not mean that we should go around moving mountains or planting sycamine trees in the sea. After all, mountains are supposed to be where they have been placed by the Lord. He does not want us messing up the scenery. Trees are not meant to be planted in the sea; the Lord never intended that.

What did our Lord mean? Surely He simply meant that whatever mountain lies in your way as an obstacle, as something insuperable, something invincible, something immovable, if you have faith as a grain of mustard seed, you can speak the word of faith to that obstacle and it will no longer be an obstacle. Maybe you will have to climb over it; maybe it will melt down at the presence of the Lord. But whatever happens, it will not be an obstacle to the fulfillment of God's purpose in your life, in your service, in your ministry, in your fellowship.

Nothing Is Impossible with God

Now you will understand this wonderful word, which I wish every one of you would write in your heart: "And nothing shall be impossible unto you." Most of us believe a whole lot of things are impossible. Some of us believe that it is impossible for husbands, wives, children, or parents to be changed. Some people believe that the situation at their place of work could never be changed. Others believe it is impossible for themselves to be changed into the likeness of the Lord. Because of their background, because of their circumstances, because of their temperament, they say that it is impossible with them. None of us would come out in the open and say it is impossible because that is not the Christian thing. We are far too well taught here for anyone to come out in the open and say, "It is impossible for me to be changed into the likeness of the Lord Jesus. It is possible with brother so and so or sister so and so, but not with me; it is impossible." But it is what we think in our heart. We say, "Not me, it is impossible. The devil has done such a work in my circumstances, he has so engineered the situation in which I am found that it is impossible for me." Nothing is impossible with God. Everything is impossible with you and with me. Not a thing will change if it is left to you or me, but with God nothing is impossible; nothing is too difficult for the Lord; nothing is too hard for the Lord.

Some people have the idea that when the Lord saved us, He did not really know us. After He brought us to a saving knowledge of Himself, then He has had shock after shock after shock. He has discovered that He has saved people who are very unyielding and very difficult. They have trying situations and circumstances, with difficult temperaments and everything that is contrary to His will. Now the Lord is in a quandary: "If only I had known this, I would never have saved them in the first place." It is ridiculous, but I put it in this way just for you to see how stupid it is. Obviously, the Lord knew you in your mother's womb. In fact, the Lord knows your whole genetic history. He knows every single thing that has gone into your make-up. There is nothing unknown to the Lord. He knows your weaknesses in a way that you do not know them. He knows what you are capable of, and still He saved you. He saved you as a hopeless, helpless sinner, and the Lord is well able to change you and to fulfill His purpose for you. He re-quires only one thing: faith as a grain of mustard seed—so small that you could overlook it, seemly so insignificant.

It Is God Who Removes Mountains

When I came to the Lord, I heard all about the victory life. We heard about it from the pulpit every Sunday. I thought they were all living it except for me. I found out years later that no one was living it. Many years later, when the pastor was more honest and I was a little older and able to ask him the question, I asked, "Did you have that victory life you preached every Sunday?" He said, "No, I preached it by faith." Those marvelous people sang with shining faces, "Victory, victory, victory," but in actual fact, nobody had any real experience of it.

I got the idea that if you had a mountain of problems in your life, you had to have a mountain of faith. In other words, however great the difficulty, you had to have the same amount of faith. I thought that if you had a mountain of obstacles or difficulties, you needed a mountain of faith a little larger in quantity than the difficulty. Then, with your mountain of faith, you bulldozed the mountain of difficulty out of the way. I would say, "Lord, I have this problem I will never come through, so I need faith like a mountain. Then I will come against this mountainous difficulty and it will disappear." It would be like driving one of those huge bulldozers and just lifting the thing out of the way, and then I would go on with the Lord. It never happened. I waited and waited and waited, but it never happened.

The Lord never gives us a mountain of faith. It would make us so self-sufficient, so independent. We would say, "I must write a book about my faith. I must tell you all about the experiences, the triumphs of faith in my life." No, the Lord does not do that kind of thing. He gives us faith so small that we can bury it, so small that we can overlook it, so insignificant, seemingly, that we would never believe that grain of faith could link us to the infinity of God. "But" you say, "it cannot be be as small as that. We need something a little more tangible, a little larger than a grain of faith. We need at least a kernel of faith, something we can see, something we can put our hands on."

I do not know how you handle a mustard seed grain. Most of the time, you can lose it; and then when you have lost it, where would you find it? It is so small, a tiny speck smaller than a flea. If you drop it, it is gone. You cannot find it anywhere. You need faith only as small as that, seemingly as insignificant as that. That little mustard seed grain of faith can link you to the almightiness of God; it can bring you into the infinity of God; it can link you to the fullness of God; it can bring you to the fathomless wisdom of God. Faith as a grain of mustard seed can change everything.

It is God who removes mountains. What a revelation it was on the day that I suddenly saw this. He made them, He put them in their place, and He can move them. You and I never move a mountain; it is God who moves mountains, but faith links me to the God who is the mountain remover. This little mustard seed of faith links us to everything God is and everything God has. We might find it very strange that it is something so small, but that is the wonder of it all.

We all have been influenced by a kind of Christian psychology. I always call it Christian Science faith. Those of you who know anything about Christian Science know it has very real miracles, but all its miracles are mind over matter. In other words, any psychologist can tell you that if you really believe something and put your whole weight behind it and say it enough times, there is a chance it could happen. If you say, "I do not have a sore finger, I do not have a sore finger, I do not have a sore finger," and you say it enough, there is a chance that you will not have a sore finger; it is gone.

I always remember the story of Winston Churchill in the war. One of the admirals in the war cabinet was a Christian Scientist, and he and Winston Churchill often would discuss Christian Science faith. It was a very cold winter's day and Winston Churchill said to the admiral, "Excuse me, you are a Christian Scientist. Would you like to sit here?" "Why?" said the admiral. Winston Churchill said, "There is a draft here." Winston Churchill always had a tendency to pneumonia and his point was that if the admiral said, "There is no draft, there is no draft, there is no draft" maybe there would not be a draft. He was not a Christian Scientist, so he thought the best thing was to get out of the draft.

This idea of faith has gone right through Christian circles. The idea is that faith is almost a kind of make-believe. If you say it enough, in the end, you kid yourself into believing it is so; and then when you really believe it is so, it will happen. This is the mentality or the concept that lies at the root of us needing an increase of faith. We need more and more of it; and as we get more and more faith, then there is a chance that it might happen. It is not Biblical faith. Biblical faith is in God who can do anything. That is the difference. The other thing is man-centered. Biblical faith is Christ-centered. That is the difference.

Living faith links you to a Person who can do anything, and that Person is the Lord Jesus. There is nothing that He cannot do. There is nothing too difficult for Him, nothing too hard for Him. Nothing is impossible with God, and faith links you to Him. It is not that somehow or other you kid yourself that this is so and, finally, it will happen and you will be amazed.

Shall Not Doubt in His Heart

Years ago, I used to suffer so much from one little verse in Mark 11. It haunted me again and again, and I could find no answer to it. Again, the Lord Jesus was speaking about faith.

"And Jesus answering saith unto them, Have faith in God. Verily I say unto you, Whosoever shall say unto this mountain, Be thou taken up and cast into the sea; and shall not doubt in his heart, but shall believe that what he saith cometh to pass; he shall have it. Therefore I say unto you, All things whatsoever ye pray and ask for, believe that ye receive them, and ye shall have them" (Mark 11:22–24).

The word that haunted me was this word "shall not doubt in his heart," because I could not understand it in my little experience and the experience of the company of believers that I was in. We had seen miracle after miracle after miracle, but the thing that most amazed me was the doubt that was in me. I never saw a miracle without doubt. The enemy would come to me and say, "Shall not doubt." I began to think: Is this Satanic? Could it be demonic? Have you ever had such a thing where you feel that maybe this is not the Lord? Of course, there were lots of Christians around us who were very much against our brother Austin Sparks, and they told us that the whole thing was of the devil, that we were deceived, we were deluded. Then I would begin to think that I did not know a single time that I had seen the Lord answer in some marvelous, miraculous way that I had not been full of doubt. So I began to think that maybe I was a special person, maybe I was one of those exceptions to the rule. But the word says, "Shall not doubt in his heart." Then, one day, the Lord said to me, "It is in your heart, not in your head." I laughed for a whole day; I could hardly believe it. You can have many doubts in your head, but it is your heart that shall have no doubt.

I remember on one occasion when we were praying about a home market garden. We had prayed so many times about this great piece of territory in the back of Halford House, claiming it for the Lord. It was worked by an old gentleman who became the key figure in the whole series on the BBC that ran for years called The Archer. His name was Dan Archer, and of course the series was Dan Archer.

We claimed this property and nothing ever happened. When we had ceased to pray, one day, he lumbered down to have a cup of tea with us, and he said, "Lance, I am old and I have a problem with my kidneys. I am going to have to let go of the market garden, and I want you to have the first offer. You have always been very good to me, and I have always promised in my heart you would have the first offer."

I looked at him with great surprise and said, "Dan, how much is it?"

"Twelve thousand pounds."

That would be about twenty thousand dollars. In those days, about thirty years ago, that was nothing. I looked at him and said, "Oh?"

He said, "I will give you a few days to work out a mortgage or get a loan."

I said, "No, we don't do that."

So he said, "How are you going to pay?"

I said, "In cash." I surprised myself when I said, "Cash."

"In cash!"

"Yes," I said, "in cash" Then I thought, What have I said?

"Okay, I will give you a few days," he said. "Think it over."

I went back into the study and got on my knees, and I said, "Lord, deliver us from this thing. If this idea of having this market garden is a dream and it is not of You, then let us let it go; but if it is of You, just let me know." In my heart, the Lord said, "You shall have it."

That evening we had a prayer meeting, and I re-member being full of doubt. We were renovating the big room, and I thought everyone was going to question where we were going to find twelve thousand pounds (twenty thousand dollars): "It is ridiculous; first, we must clear the renovation of the room, and then we can think of it." I thought there was going to be trouble. We prayed, and when I told everyone all about it, we prayed more. Everyone said that we must go ahead. "But," I said, "we do not have the money." They said that we must go ahead.

I told them that they must not tell anyone about this because there were all kinds of big businesses that would give three or four times this amount of money for that very valuable piece of ground in the center of Richmond, Surrey. Everyone said they would not say anything. Early the next morning, I had a phone call from a lady who lived about eighty miles away. She said, "Lance, I am phoning you about the market garden."

I said, "How did you know?"

"Never mind," she said.

I said, "I mind very much. Someone in the prayer meeting has phoned you and told you. It is absolutely wrong because we were all sworn together not to speak to anyone outside the company."

She said, "Just wait; come down off your high horse. I woke up this morning at 5 o'clock and all I could hear in my heart was: "The garden, the garden; buy the garden." I have been phoning all around the south of England trying to find where there is a garden for sale. I did not find anyone till I found so and so."

She said, "Oh, Lance has told you about the garden."

So she said, "No, the Lord spoke to me early this morning."

Then she said, "Oh, I should not have said anything. You better phone Lance yourself."

And she did. The most amazing thing is that we had twelve thousand pounds in cash within twenty-four hours. That was years ago. Of course, its value would be more today.

What I am trying to tell you is this: "Shall not doubt in his heart." I had so many doubts in my head, but in my heart I had the strangest sense. When the Lord said, "You shall have it," I burst out laughing. That is when I first knew how Sarah laughed over Isaac. The Lord had such humor that when Isaac was born, He said, "Call him Isaac—laughter."

Faith is the linking of us to all God's provision—all the fulfillment of God's purpose and Word, all God's fullness, all God's power. Isn't it tragic that we are so spiritually poor? I am not talking about physical riches, but we are spiritually poor because we do not know how to exercise faith.

Hall of Faith

I think of Hebrews 11, that marvelous catalogue of saints. The amazing thing is that the writer only touched on certain things by the Holy Spirit. He could have extended this into another letter, almost. But those saints were linked by a grain of mustard seed faith to the greatness of God and found themselves in the fulfillment of the purpose of God. It was by faith, by faith, by faith, by faith.

Abraham

What would have happened when the Lord appeared to Abraham if he had never obeyed? By faith he obeyed. He went out, not even knowing where he was going. According to our tradition,

Abraham came from one of the great aristocratic families of Ur of the Chaldees. He was not, as the liberal theologians tell us, some wandering, illiterate Bedouin shepherd. He came from one of the great aristocratic families whose business of making idols had made them wealthy. Abraham's father, Terah, and the rest of the family had a very nice business in making idols. One day, the God of glory appeared to Abraham, and in that vision of the God of glory, Abraham saw the Messiah. That is what it says in the New Testament: Jesus said, "He saw My day and rejoiced." He not only saw the Messiah, he saw the city of God; we are not told how, but something happened to Abraham. From his education, his sophistication, his riches, his standard of living, he went out, not knowing where he was going. We all know this because it is in the Bible, but can you imagine it! He just walked out. Of course, he had been told to leave, to get out of his father's house; but he took his father with him, which was trouble. He also took Lot, and as Mr. Sparks used to say, "He was a lot of trouble." He should never have taken them; the purpose could not be fulfilled in them.

God spoke to Abraham about a land and said it was all his; but he never owned any part of it except one cave, Machpelah in Ephron, where he is buried. He looked for the city which has foundations, and he never dwelt in it. When the Lord took him out on that wonderful middle eastern night and told him to look up, he saw the stars. God said, "Your seed shall be as the stars and the sand of the seashore for multitude." He lived to almost 100 years of age and did not have a child. Finally, he ended up with two sons, but one of them was a mistake. The amazing thing is that it was by faith. Oh, there were collapses of faith in Abraham, but it was by faith that suddenly he was joined to God. I wonder whether

Abraham ever realized that he would become a household word, that he would become the great symbol of faith, that he would be called the father of all who believe. That simple faith, like a grain of mustard seed, took him out of the great, sophisticated city complex he lived in into the purpose of God.

It is exactly the same with you and me. It is faith that brings us into understanding, into vision, and our lives are never the same again.

Jacob

Jacob's problem was not the same as Abraham's; Jacob's problem was Jacob. That was the greatest problem Jacob had. Actually, people always think of Jacob as a supplanter, a deceiver, a twister, and of course, he was. But somehow or other in Christian circles, Jacob has been put over as a weak, spineless, anemic, home-loving, unattractive man. I do not think it is a true picture. I think it is very interesting that from the very beginning, Jacob had a hunger for the things of God. Whatever failings he had, whatever faults he had, he put a tremendous value on the birthright and the blessing.

As for Esau, I often think he would have been a very straight fellow. People portray him as a dolt, as some kind of athletic, brainless monster with a huge appetite. I do not think so. I think Esau was a very straight man. Jacob was not a straight man. Esau knew what he wanted, and he had no time for the things of God. He did not put any value on the birthright or the blessing. He came right out in the open with it: "I am not interested." Jacob stole the birthright and the blessing.

The last picture we have of Jacob in the Bible is the one in Hebrews 11, where it says, "By faith, he blessed the two sons of Joseph, leaning on his staff." Jacob was not a blessing; he robbed people of the blessing. Wherever he went, he took it from them. He robbed his twin brother; he robbed his old, blind father; he made his mother very unhappy for the last days of her life and she never saw him again; he robbed his uncle, Laban. Of course, it was business, but the way he did it was by robbing them of everything. Some people say that the Lord had already said the birthright and the blessing were to come to him, but it was the way he did it.

When God brought him to Jabbok, He changed him. He was given another name, Israel—"Prince with God." The Bible says the pure in heart shall see the Lord. Jacob saw the Lord. How do you explain that? You certainly would not call Jacob pure in heart; maybe Abraham, maybe Moses, but never Jacob. But the way the Lord measures is quite different. Somehow there was something in the heart of Jacob in spite of all his crookedness that was pure. When God changed Jacob, the one who robbed everyone of their blessing, he became the one who blessed. Pharaoh, the greatest potentate in antiquity, bowed before him, and Jacob laid his hands on his head and blessed him—and it was a blessing. Jacob blessed his twelve sons, one by one, with tremendous insight. He blessed the two sons of Joseph, leaning on his staff because God had crippled him. It was by faith.

Something happened in Jacob. That little grain of mustard seed faith was there from the beginning. That is why he wanted the birthright; that is why he wanted the blessing; that is why when the Lord appeared to him, he bargained with the Lord and said if He would look after him, he would build God a house and give Him a tenth of everything—as if the Lord needed it. There was a grain of faith in that. Jacob's problem was Jacob; but with all his crookedness, because he sought for the Lord, the Lord met him and changed him.

Moses

Moses was so different. He really did have an education. He was sophisticated; he was privileged; he be-longed to the elite; he was Pharaoh's daughter's son. He was the grandson of Pharaoh, groomed for the palace. In every way his education, his instruction, his discipline was royal. From our Jewish sources, we know that Moses was a great athlete. We also know that he was a hero of the Ethiopian campaign and the Libyan campaign. He was highly decorated and a popular hero of the people of Egypt. All this makes us realize how much Moses gave up. It was by faith that he forsook the riches of Egypt and esteemed the reproach of the Messiah greater riches. It is an amazing story. For forty years, this sophisticated, educated, Egyptian hero, this grandson of Pharaoh kept sheep and goats in the desert. The Egyptians had a horror of sheep and goats; they actually did not like shepherds. That was the lowest of the low in Egyptian society. The grandson of Pharaoh was keeping sheep—not for one year, not for two years, but for forty years. For most of us, that is a lifetime. We would be retired by then.

At the end of forty years, he saw that thorn bush burning with fire. When he came near and looked down in it, he heard the voice of God: "Take off the shoes from your feet; the ground whereon you stand is holy." Moses said, "Who are You?" The Lord said, "I AM that I AM. Tell them I AM has sent you."

I have heard some tremendous messages on this "I AM that I AM" that absolutely dazzled one's brain and fascinated one with the infinity of God and the power of God. But years ago, I heard a little old Irish man, an evangelist, who had been used by the Lord to bring so many of the Irish to Himself. His name was Johnny Cochran. He stood up at the Lord's table and said: "All the messages and sermons I have ever heard on 'I AM that I AM' have left me stone cold until, one day, the Lord said to me, 'Johnny, I AM—fill in what you need. Do you need grace? I AM grace. Do you need power? I AM power. Do you need authority? I AM your authority. Do you need love? I AM your love. I AM everything you need. The infinite God, the all-powerful God—I AM at your disposal. You are the thorn bush; I AM the fire. Let the fire get into the old, dead thorn bush and we will make history."

By faith, Moses went back to Pharaoh and challenged the mightiest and greatest super-power of his day. He saw the whole thing brought down to zero and the purpose of God fulfilled. "Faith as a grain of mustard seed."

Joshua

I think of Joshua. I think of those twelve spies who went into the land and they all saw the same things. Ten came back saying that the land was filled with giants and cities walled up to heaven: "It is impossible; we are dead meat." Two said, "No; God has said we shall go up and take this land. It is our land; it is a promised land; it is our inheritance. We shall go in and the Lord will be with us." By faith, they inherited.

A Living, Working Faith

What a tremendous thing this faith as a grain of mustard seed is! What we need is a living, working faith. It is interesting that the Lord Jesus said, "If you have faith as a grain of mustard seed and shall say...." It is faith that works. It is not in our head. It is faith that is expressed. Then, in the expression of that little grain of mustard seed faith, you are linked to the infinity of God. Then the impossible happens. The Red Sea is parted; water comes out of the rock; Pharaoh's crack, elite commandos disappear.

Do you have such faith? Now if you are saved, you must have faith, because by grace you have been saved through faith; and that not of yourselves, it is the gift of God. Somewhere, you have shelved your little grain of faith. You have buried it— sometimes under theology, sometimes under a spiritual facade. Sometimes the knowledge has grown but the faith is inoperative. That faith as a grain of mustard seed must have been given to you and it is still there. You may be ignoring it, overlooking it; you may have shelved it; you may have buried it, but it is still there or else you could not be saved.

How to Know a Living, Working Faith

How can I know such a living, working faith? It is only by looking unto Jesus. It is interesting that in this great catalogue of saints, which unfortunately is divided by chapters and verses, we suddenly find this word: "Therefore let us also, seeing we are compassed about with so great a cloud of witnesses, lay aside every weight, and the sin which doth so easily beset us, and let us run with patience the race that is set before us, looking unto Jesus the author and [finisher] of our faith" (Hebrews 12:1–2a). So it is the Lord Jesus who authorizes faith, who brings faith to birth in our heart. It is the Lord Jesus who gives finishing faith. Sometimes we need faith to begin; sometimes we need faith to finish. But whatever faith we need, it is only when we see the Lord Jesus that that faith is operative. Why is it that the faith that is like a little grain of mustard seed in our hearts and lives is not operative? Why doesn't it function? The reason that it does not operate in you or in me is because we are not seeing the Lord. When we see the Lord, faith spontaneously functions. All we need is obedience.

That is why I read those two stories in Matthew's gospel. When I first began to read the Bible at 13 years of age, I had a thousand questions. One of my questions was why we have two stories about the Lord and boats. Of course, the liberals tell us it is the same story, it just got muddled up. Different people told the same story; one said one thing and one said the other and both got shoved into the gospel. Of course, I cannot accept that. I do not believe that type of nonsense.

The Lord Stops the Storm

The first story is very interesting, and this is how I see it. The Lord got into the boat with his disciples, going to the other side, and immediately, he went into a deep sleep. Now I think this is very unlike our Lord; He normally is so caring and thoughtful. Why did He fall into such a deep sleep, especially when He knew very well that a great storm was coming? Waves were crashing over the boat. People say that it was the humanity of the Lord Jesus. Humanity of the Lord Jesus! We have had storms that are like the blitz in London, and I have been with people who have slept through the whole thing. I could have been murdered right next to them, and they would have woken up in the morning and found me dead. They never woke once. I just cannot believe that our Lord Jesus slept so deeply. No; it was deliberate! I think it was deliberate. He went fast asleep, knowing very well that a great storm was upon them. He may even have said, "Oh Father, just make that storm so big," and the waves came right over the boat.

They said, "He is worn out." They bailed out the water, but it was coming in faster than they were bailing it out. Then they decided they had better wake Him. They shook Him and He woke up and said, "Yes?"

They said, "Master, are You not even a little bothered? We are perishing."

"Oh," He said. They were in such a panic. He stood up and said, "Silent, be still," and the storm stopped.

I have a theory that our Lord really was going to teach them how to walk on the sea, but He knew very well they were going to panic. There was no way He could do it. So they had a wonderful experience. The Lord stopped the storm dead, just like that. When the Lord does that in our lives, isn't it wonderful? We worship Him. But we have not learned a lot. All we have learned is that the Lord can stop a storm in our lives, that He has power and authority; but what have we learned in our own being? I do not think we have learned so much.

Faith to Walk Through the Storm

The second time our Lord took them down to the boat and constrained them to get into the boat. That is a very strong word.

He really forced them. He marched them to the boat and told them to go over to the other side and He would send the people away. I suppose they said He could not do it alone, but He said He was going to do it alone, and for them to go to the other side. Then He sent the multitudes away. I do not know how He managed that, knowing the crowds with all their questions and everything else. He went up alone, very unconcerned, and prayed. I wonder what He prayed. Did He pray for a storm? Certainly, before very long, a storm blew up, and those poor disciples were rowing and they were sinking, getting nowhere. Then suddenly, through all the sound of the wind and waves, and the spray of the waves, they saw something like an apparition. Mark said, "He went as to go beyond the boat." So it is not like Matthew, where it sounds like He went straight into the boat. No; He went right past the boat. They looked and said it was a ghost. Then one of the others said, "No; I think it is the Lord."

I can hear one of them saying, Thomas probably, "Well, that is funny. Why doesn't He come over to us? Why does He go beyond us?"

Then Peter said, "Lord, is it You?"

The Lord said through the sound of the waves and wind, "Yes, it is Me."

Then Peter said, "Tell me to come to You."

The Lord Jesus said, "Come."

Peter got out of the boat, down onto the water, and he walked on the water. He never for a moment thought, "What am I doing? I am walking on the water." He had never been to a theological seminary and taken the five steps in walking on water. He had never read a book on How to Walk On Water. He had never done it in his life. As far as Peter was concerned, it was impossible for a man to walk on the water. I have no doubt that as a fisherman, he knew very well that you do not walk on water; it was his milieu. But suddenly, he was walking on the water.

Listen carefully: He saw the Lord, he heard the Lord, and he did the impossible. He saw the Lord, he recognized the Lord, he heard the Lord's word "Come," and he obeyed. Did he think, "Have I got faith? Have I got enough faith to climb out of this boat and walk on the water? Have I got enough faith to walk in spite of these waves and this wind?" He never thought about it. He saw the Lord, he heard the Lord, and he obeyed the Lord—and he did the impossible. That is how it works. That is why faith is not a self-conscious thing. You do not think about it. You see the Lord, you hear the Lord, you obey the Lord, and immediately, the impossible becomes possible.

Somewhere along the way, at some point, Peter saw the waves and the wind. He was walking on the water toward the Lord, and perhaps a great wave came between him and the Lord. Suddenly, he thought, "Oh my goodness, I am walking on water," and he sank. The moment he looked at the waves and heard the wind, he said, "What am I doing? Have I got faith enough for this?" And he sank. He cried, "Lord, save me!" The Lord caught him and said, "Why did you doubt, oh ye of little faith." How does living faith work? It works by seeing the Lord.

What is wrong with our sight? What sin has interfered with our sight? What compromise has interfered with our sight? Why are we not seeing the Lord? Our Lord Jesus said to the church of Laodicea, "I council you [or I advise you] to buy of me eyesalve to anoint your eyes, that you may see" (see Revelation 3:18b). He did not want them just to see their wretchedness or their nakedness or their worldliness. He wanted them to see Himself; then they would know their condition.

It is always a good thing when we see the Lord and discover our condition. We need to ask the Lord for this spiritual eye-salve that touches our eyes so that we are re-centered on the Lord Jesus, so that we see the Lord Jesus. What matters if there is a storm? What matters if the waves are huge? What matters if the wind roars as long as we can see the Lord? Then we shall learn how to walk on the storm. That is a far greater lesson to learn than merely the greatness and authority of the Lord Jesus stopping a storm. To learn how to walk in a storm, through a storm, on a storm is a tremendous lesson. Then we shall not become destabilized, we shall not lose our balance, we shall not lose our poise. Whatever comes in the last phase of world history, we shall have learned, by keeping our eyes on the Lord Jesus and obeying His word, how to walk through the storm. May the Lord touch our hearts and do something for us. We do not need more faith; we need to see the Lord.

Shall we pray?

Father, You know the condition of every single one of us. You know the various problems we have with our spiritual sight. Oh Lord, touch us. It is not more faith we need; it is to see You. When we see You, Lord, we know something will happen—just like when Abraham saw the God of glory, and when Jacob said, "I have seen the face of the Lord and I have lived." Lord, work in our lives. Whatever may mar our vision of You, whatever has come between us and You, will You touch it? Will you grant that as we see You and as we obey Your word, we shall learn how to walk on the stormy waters? Father, be with us. Come to us in all our need and meet us at the point where we are. We ask it in the name of our Lord Jesus. Amen.

3.
The Trial of Faith

1 Peter 1:3–9

Blessed be the God and Father of our Lord Jesus Christ, who according to his great mercy begat us again unto a living hope by the resurrection of Jesus Christ from the dead, unto an inheritance incorruptible, and undefiled, and that fadeth not away, reserved in heaven for you, who by the power of God are guarded through faith unto a salvation ready to be revealed in the last time. Wherein ye greatly rejoice, though now for a little while, if need be, ye have been put to grief in manifold trials, that the proof of your faith, being more precious that gold that perisheth though it is proved by fire, may be found unto praise and glory and honor at the revelation of Jesus Christ: whom not having seen ye love; on whom, though now ye see him not, yet believing, ye rejoice greatly with joy unspeakable and full of glory: receiving the end of your faith, even the salvation of your souls.

Luke 22:31

Simon, Simon, behold, Satan asked to have you, that he might sift you as wheat: but I made supplication [prayer] for thee, that thy faith fail not; and do thou, when once thou hast turned again, establish thy brethren.

II Timothy 2:13

If we are faithless, he abideth faithful; for he cannot deny himself.

Shall we pray?

Lord, when we come to the ministry of Your word, we are so inadequate, unprofitable to be a channel for You to speak. But Lord, we want to thank You that You have made a provision for us in all our weakness and unworthiness. You have provided an anointing for speaking, for the translating, and for the hearing; and we want to avail ourselves of that anointing. We know it is all of grace; it is all of Yourself. Therefore, by faith, we stand into that anointing together that You will take this time and make it a meeting with Yourself and deposit something within our lives that can never be taken away. Cause that word to take root in us and grow and bear much fruit, and we shall give You all the praise and all the glory. In the name of our Messiah, the Lord Jesus. Amen.

A Sinner Becomes a Praise to God

I want to consider this matter of the trial of faith. That is the old King James rendering of this word in I Peter 1:7: "The trial of your faith, being much more precious than of gold that perisheth, though it be tried with fire, might be found unto praise and honor and glory at the [revelation] of Jesus Christ."

The testing or trying of genuine faith is a principle with God. The Lord always tries or tests real faith. Where there is head faith or academic faith, He leaves it. It is nothing to do with Him. It never came from Him in the first place, so He does not bother with it. But where there is real faith which is the gift of God, born in the human heart, He tests it and tries it.

When Peter wrote this first letter, he wrote out of deep, costly, shattering experience. He spoke words of comfort to strengthen those that he believed could go through something like he had gone through. When he spoke about "the trial of your faith," Peter knew, perhaps better than anyone, something about the proving of a living faith.

What a beautiful word this is: "That it may be found unto praise and honor and glory." Living faith is the only thing that can bring a sinner, saved by the grace of God, to the place where he becomes a praise to the Lord. For all eternity, angels and the multitude of the redeemed will praise God for what He has done in your life. They see that this faith brought you into something of God that could never be taken away and changed you into His likeness and glory. It actually brought you to the place where there is something of Christ in you, something of the nature of Christ in you, something of the life of Christ in you so that there is a capacity for glory and honor. Honor speaks of reward and status. Where there has been living faith, enduring faith, overcoming faith, finally, there will be honor. "Praise, honor, and glory at the revelation of Jesus Christ." What a marvelous phrase this is!

Born Again to a Living Hope

I want to underline a few things Peter said in 1 Peter 1:3–5: "Born again to a living hope." Some people think being born again is the hope. But we are born again to a living hope. In other words, our birth is but the initial experience, the introduction, the beginning. The Lord has brought us into something, and the goal is a living hope. Have you ever realized that when God saved you, He had a goal, an objective, something that He saved you for, something for which He has brought you to a second birth that you might enter into?

Resurrection of Jesus Christ

"By the resurrection of Jesus Christ from the dead." Isn't that wonderful too when you think about it! It is not just His atoning work on the cross by which we know forgiveness and cleansing and justification, but by the resurrection of Jesus Christ from the dead, we are joined to God in Him—a living hope.

An Inheritance Incorruptible

"To an inheritance incorruptible, unsoiled, and un-fading." That is a wonderful word. We all fade. It is a shock each year when I see friends and they have a few more wrinkles, a little more fading. Every one of us is actually fading as we get older. We have corruptible bodies. It is marvelous to know the incorruptible life of the Lord in our bodies, overcoming even the corruption that is within us through sin. But thank God that while everything around us is corruptible, soiled, or fading, we have an inheritance incorruptible. It cannot be corrupted; it cannot be soiled. It is beyond the touch of being soiled or spoiled, defiled. It is unfading. It is simply wonderful to think that everything God is doing in my life and your life and in our fellowship together is producing materials that are out of the touch of the enemy— gold, precious stone, pearl—out of which the city is created, out of which the bride is produced. This is something that is actually worked in us and produced in us on earth in very corruptible circumstances, very fading circumstances, often very defiled situations. Here we are as human beings, sinners saved by grace; and yet in these conditions on this earth, in a world that lies in the hands of the evil one, God is producing something in us which is all to do with an inheritance incorruptible, unsoiled, and unfading. It is marvelous! Few believers seem to know anything about this inheritance. Paul prayed that the eyes of our hearts may be opened, that a spirit of wisdom and revelation may be given to us, that we may know what is the hope of His calling and what are the riches of the glory of His inheritance in the saints.

Reserved in Heaven for You

"Reserved in heaven for you." It is not just for Watchman Nee, or Martin Luther, or the apostle Paul or the apostle Peter, but for you. You! You! It is reserved for you. What a tragedy when no material is going up, when we never cooperate with the Lord so that He can produce the kind of material that is incorruptible, unsoiled, and does not fade, reserved for you. I love that word reserved. We all want to reserve things. Whenever we go to an event or restaurant, we like to book a table or make a reservation. Only a fool tries to go on flights, especially to some countries, without a reservation. You have to make a reservation. But what a wonderful thing that God Himself has reserved something for you. He has reserved this inheritance for you.

Guarded by the Power of God

"Who by the power of God are guarded through faith unto a salvation ready to be revealed in the last time." Think of the power of God. God spoke the Word and it was done. He said, "Let there be light," and there was light. Everything we see in this universe came through the Word of God. He spoke and it was done. Oh, the power of God! Again and again, in the Old Covenant, we are reminded that He made the heavens and the earth. We often forget this—that He made the heavens and the earth and everything that is within them. Oh, the infinite power of God is unbelievable!

Think of the power of God that came upon Mary when she conceived and bore the Savior of the world. What power! What unbelievable power! How unbelievably incredible! How did the Lord do it? It is something beyond even the greatest in spiritual intelligence in the world to understand the incarnation. Yet, it was the power of God that came upon Mary and brought to birth the Lord Jesus.

I think of the work on the cross. In all the weakness of the Lord Jesus being nailed to the cross, it was the very power of God so that when He died, something went right through the very universe. It shuttered; it darkened, as if for a single moment a sword went through the very heart of God, and everything shuttered for a moment or two. When the Lord Jesus, who knew no sin, became sin for us that we might become the righteousness of God, it was the power of God. It is so amazing!

Can you take it in that you can be guarded by the power of God? God has committed Himself, covenanted Himself to you. You and I are little bits of human debris, little bits of human flotsam and jetsam. We are really rubbish. I do not know if you have come to that conclusion, but if you live long enough, you will come to it. We are just little bits of rubbish. We are so insignificant, so unworthy, so unprofitable. The more we know the Lord, the less profitable we seem to be. Yet, God has covenanted Himself to you and to me. He knows you by name. He did not save you as a unit, as a number, as some nameless unit in a great mass. He saved you because He knows you. He knew you before you were born. He knows everything about you, and He loves you. This God who created all things, with whom nothing is impossible, has covenanted Himself with His whole power to you. He says, "All My power is at your disposal, not merely to save you, not merely to bring you to a new birth, but to keep you, to guard you so that you may grow and be changed into the likeness of My Son and finally stand before Me blameless, without fault in exceeding joy." It is the power of God. If some security core unit would offer their help in keeping me, I would be quite thankful, but it is nothing compared to the power of God. What can the security core unit do when it comes to Satan? They do not even know, hardly, who he is; they would not know how to defend against him. But what about the power of God committed to you and to me to keep us? It is unbelievable.

"Who by the power of God are guarded through faith." If you and I do not have a living, working faith, the power of God is shelved. That is the strategic and vital nature of a living, working faith. God puts His power at your disposal to guard you, to keep you, and to bring you to that inheritance incorruptible, unsoiled, unfading; but if you do not have living faith which will join you to Him, then you are not kept.

Proven Faith

Peter points out to us that this kind of faith has to be tried. The old King James Version used the word "the trial of your faith." But in our day, a trial has a very negative feeling. We feel that a trial is an inquisition, an interrogation, a kind of negative, dark thing. We feel that a trial is finding out what should not be there; but actually, the word trial means to find out that you are not guilty. It is to prove the truth about a matter. A trial is neither negative nor positive; it is there to discover what is the truth. But because we have got this idea that a trial is a very negative thing, I think some of the other versions are much better. The 1901 American Standard Version says, "The proof of your faith." Actually, the word could be translated: "The testing of your faith," or "The trial of your faith." Mr. Sparks always said that he liked the word "the proving"—not just the proof—of your faith. "The proving of your faith, being more precious than gold that perisheth, may be found unto praise and glory and honor at the revelation of Jesus Christ." This is a principle with God.

If you are the possessor of a living, working faith, it will be tested; it will be tried; it will be proved. The beautiful thing about the word proved is that it has a wonderfully positive feel about it. In other words, you are proving something; you are not destroying something. You are proving that it works, that it is present, that it is there. Every true believer, at some point, will come into this proving or testing of their faith.

God never tries in a believer what is not there; He proves what is there. I will say it again: God never tries what is not there; He proves what is there. In other words, if there is living, working faith, He will destroy all the pseudo faith, the counterfeit faith, the self-manufactured faith, all the accretions, all the additions; and He will purify that faith that joins you to Him. He will prove that it works. He proves it by the situations, the circumstances, the experiences that He brings you into. So we see the necessity of chastening, the necessity of pruning, the necessity of discipline and testing. It is always a sign that there is true faith.

If you have never had a testing of your faith, it means that God cannot touch you because He is afraid that if He puts you to the test, He will lose you. You are not even at the point where He can prove; it is too dangerous. Here is the amazing and comforting thing: If you are going through trials, if you are going through very dark and difficult experiences, it is because God has gifted you with living, working faith and He is proving it.

Illustrations of Living Faith

Job

The Bible is filled with illustrations, for example Job. There was no one more perfect than Job. I often hear people speak about Job and how self-righteousness he was, so full of pride; but God never said that at all. When Satan came into the presence of God, He said, "Have you seen My servant Job? He is perfect." Have you ever heard of such a thing?

The Lord said to Satan, "Look at My servant Job."

Satan said, "Let me have him."

"Why should I let you have him?" the Lord said.

Satan said, "Because he has everything. He has wonderful sons, wonderful daughters, a wonderful wife. He has great prosperity. You have blessed all his cattle, all his camels, all his horses and asses. You have multiplied everything. His olive trees yield a massive yield. His vines are full of grapes. Of course, he is perfect." Now that is not necessarily true because many people who are blessed are not perfect; they forget the Lord. Job never forgot the Lord. He offered sacrifices, he worshiped the Lord and he prayed. Then Satan said to God, "You let me have him."

God Uses Satan for the Trying of Our Faith

Here is our first lesson. In the trial of faith, Satan is the great agent. God always uses Satan. That is why C. T. Studd once said, "There is no greater servant of God than Satan." God always uses Satan to do good. I know some people are terribly shocked by this. Think of the end of Job. It was all Satan's work. He stripped Job, first, of all his sons, all his daughters, all his possessions, and finally himself. It was all Satan's work. When he was totally stripped of everything, to begin with, Job said, "The Lord has given, the Lord has taken away; blessed be the name of the Lord." Then his dear beloved wife came to him and said, "Why don't you curse God?

After all, you had all these wonderful things, and what has God done? He is not worth believing in." But Job was unshakable.

Job's Friends

Then came his friends. Satan often uses believing friends. If these dear friends had only kept their big mouths shut—but could they? Impossible! It is a very strange thing that as soon as you get into trouble, you will always get people telling you why. To begin with, they are quiet and sympathetic; but after a while, they will write you or they will tell you why you are in trouble— why this, why that. It is quite amazing. We all do it to one another. His friends came and sat with him in quietness for a while. That was as much as their spirituality could bear. They waited for the Lord to do something to poor Job and for him to come out in the open with his confession, and when he did not play ball, they started. They were going to make up for the lack of the Holy Spirit.

Some of the things that Job's friends said are absolutely marvelous. I have heard many sermons preached on the words of Job's friends, although at the end of it the Lord said they had not said the thing which was right. Yet I have heard the most wonderful things said: "Lay thou thy treasure in the dust and the Lord shall be thy treasure and precious silver unto thee." That was said by one of the friends of Job. One of them, Eliphaz, was a little better than the others, but the Lord said that all of them had not said the right thing. It was the trial of Job's faith.

The friends said wonderful things, Biblical things, doctrinally sound things; and Job said a whole lot of things that were very wrong. The more they prodded him, the more he said: "Well,

I do not know. The Lord is like this to me, but why, I do not understand." After a while, he began to say, "The Lord has trampled all over me and I do not understand. He has got an argument with me; why doesn't He kill me?" Job said some very wrong things, but at the end, it was Job whom the Lord brought through; and the Lord was so angry with the friends of Job that He said to Job, "Pray for them or I will judge them."

The End of Job

There is that wonderful word of Job at the end when he said, "I have up to now only heard with the hearing of my ear [secondhand], but now my eyes see." It was the trial or proving of Job. It was a tough trial, but what did it prove? It proved that in Job there was something of God so pure, so genuine, so born of God that when Satan had moved in, and Job's believing friends, it could not destroy what was of God. In the end, Job came through with more than he ever had before. This is a very interesting example because it is an example not of the collapse of faith; but here was a man who really trusted the Lord, whose reactions and responses were absolutely honoring to the Lord, yet the Lord had so much to do in Job till he came into a new place.

Abraham

Abraham is the great illustration and example of faith, but have you ever thought of him in the trial of faith? You know that the Lord said to Abraham, "Look north, look east, look south, look west; all that you see I give to you. Look up and see the stars. Can you count them? Your seed will be more in number than those stars." Dear Abraham—then came the proving of his faith.

He had gone out of Ur of the Chaldees with a living, working faith that joined him to God. He took Terah his father and Lot with him, and he had to wait until the Lord delivered him from both of them before he entered Canaan. Then came the trial of his faith—famine. Sometimes, famine comes from God. A famine came—one year, two years—the former and latter rains failed, and their whole livelihood was threatened. He had great flocks of sheep, goats, camels, asses, and they had to find food. What could they do? I do not know where it came from, but he heard there was plenty in Egypt, and so came the test: "Of course, it is more important for you, Abraham, to live, isn't it? Where is this son? No son! If you die of starvation, there will not be a son. Go down to Egypt. It will only be for a little time."

Abraham Goes down to Egypt

Abraham went down into Egypt. He must have been a quite remarkable man because Pharaoh soon heard about him and said he would like to meet the new guest, the new tourist. A meeting was arranged, and of course, Sarah met Pharaoh. Sarah must have been incredibly beautiful and graceful because as soon as Pharaoh saw Sarah, he was staggered. Of course, he did not look at her too long. That was not done, but he noticed all the same. She was really a beauty. But Abraham had noticed that look; and when Pharaoh asked him who she was, he said, "Oh, she is my sister." Actually, it was half-truth; she was his half sister. She was the daughter of his father but not the daughter of his mother (see Genesis 20:12). Poor Abraham never should have gotten into that mess. Pharaoh sent his chamberlain and other officials to see Abraham to arrange the marriage to Sarah.

Can you imagine! Abraham had to look as if he was very pleased. Obviously, he could not look upset. Now he was caught; it was the trial of his faith. Poor, poor Abraham. What humor the Lord has!

Pharaoh never touched Sarah. We do not know why. In the old days, they made pacts and alliances that way, and perhaps Pharaoh wanted to make some alliance with these people from the mountainous country north of Egypt. All we do know is that, after a while, all kinds of things happened in Pharaoh's household until, in the end, the magician said to him, "Something is very wrong," and they decided that it had to do with his new wife.

Finally, Pharaoh asked Abraham why he had done this, that he had had trouble in his household ever since Sarah had stepped into it. She had not done anything, she had not argued; but he had had trouble after trouble. Abraham must have thought he was going to be executed or something terrible was going to happen to him, that there was going to be a war or something, but the Lord got him out of it. That was the trial of his faith; it was the collapse of faith. Then of course, later on, he went back to them.

There are a lot of times when God tells us to go down into Egypt. He took Jacob down to Egypt; that was the will of the Lord. There are other times when, like Elijah, the Lord can keep you alive in a time of famine by ravens, which are non-kosher birds. Elijah was a good Jew, and with a non-kosher bird bringing food, he could have questioned it and said, "I wonder what this is." But he was kept alive for three years by the ravens bringing morsels. Those non-kosher birds were used by God to bring food to His servant, and there was a brook that never failed. God kept him alive. What an experience Elijah had of the miraculous provision of God. Abraham could have had that hundreds of years before, but his faith collapsed and he went down into Egypt.

Abraham Listens to His Wife

The same thing happened over the child. Abraham had this wonderful promise of a child: "All the families of the world will be blessed in your seed;" but he had no seed. He waited and waited, and he really believed. He got older and older and older and older and older. Worse still, Sarah got older and older and older and older, till he was ninety-nine and she was not far behind that. Then he began to wonder: "Have I misunderstood? Has the Lord some other way of doing things?" They had a little talk. Sometimes it was a good thing when Abraham harkened to Sarah, and sometimes it was a bad thing. On this occasion, he listened to Sarah and she said: "My dear, it is perfectly clear what the Lord is saying to us. You could probably still produce a child but I cannot. What about my handmaid, Hagar?" This was quite the common thing in that day.

"Isn't she an Egyptian?" Abraham asked.

Sarah said, "Yes, we got her when we went down into Egypt. She is a nice girl. I think she is healthy, and I think she would produce a good child."

Abraham said: "I see what you mean; this is common sense. God has given us common sense. How stupid of me. I have been waiting all these years for some mysterious, miraculous provision, and of course, God has given us human beings common sense." Thus came Ishmael. It was a collapse of faith that is still with us today.

In the end, the Lord came back to Abraham and had a meal with him, and it was not a kosher meal because they had milk and meat all mixed up together. Suddenly, the Lord said to Abraham, "At the right time, within a short period, your wife will bear a son." Sarah was in the tent behind the flap, and she burst out laughing. We have one of the funniest stories in the Old Testament in which the Lord is speaking to Sarah through the tent flap: "Why did you laugh?" He said. "I did not laugh," she said, "I am so sorry." But she had a son and she called him "laughter" because the Lord told her to do so. It was the collapse of faith, yet God remained faithful. In spite of Abraham's collapse of faith, God brought him right through.

Joseph

There is a very amazing little word about Joseph in Psalm 105: "[Joseph's] feet they hurt with fetters: he was laid in chains of iron [his soul entered into the iron], until the time that his word [the word of the Lord to Joseph] came to pass, the word of [the Lord] tried him" (vv. 18–9).

Joseph was in the dungeon. He knew those vision dreams that God had given him were to be absolutely fulfilled. He had been a very arrogant, precocious young man; but he was his father's favorite. Those dreams, which were given by God, were prophetic, and they were to be absolutely fulfilled. When he went into the dungeon, God gave him understanding of what would happen with Egypt and all the rest. Somehow, Satan came to him, but it was the Word of the Lord that tried him. In the dungeon, as his soul entered into iron, the Word of the Lord came to him again and again. I imagine Joseph was tempted to say, "I think it was

an imagination I had. I think it was my pride of presumption."
I am sure that Satan said to him, "You are so proud and you
have gotten yourself into this mess. You are so presumptuous,
so precocious, so proud that you deserve this. You think that
God is going to do something with you." But he believed God,
and in the end, he became the savior of Egypt and the savior of
the Jewish people. It was the trial of his faith.

Moses

Moses was one of the elite. He was educated; he had status;
he was privileged as Pharaoh's grandson. Everything about Moses
was magnificent—his athleticism, his military prowess, the fact
that he was a popular folk hero in Egypt. I have no doubt that all
the things that we know from our tradition about Moses are true.
When that Hebrew slave, who was probably a strong, young man,
was fighting with that strong, young Egyptian, Moses stepped in
and killed him. He could not have been very weak because he was
trained in martial arts. After Moses killed him, he did not know
what to do, but he thought he had better bury him in order to get
rid of the evidence. Then began the trial of his faith.

Do you not think that his mother and father spoke to him about
his unbelievable deliverance and that maybe God had something
special for him? This was a Hebrew brought up as an Egyptian in
the royal house as Pharaoh's grandson. Surely they might have
thought God had a purpose for him, that he might be the deliverer
they were looking for.

When Moses fled into the desert, I have no doubt he thought
it would just be a few months, maybe a year at the most. It was to
be forty years—one year after the other—one boring year after

boring year. After all his experience in Pharaoh's court, all his experience in the Egyptian army, all his experience in Egypt, what was he doing keeping sheep and goats on the backside of the desert? Poor Moses. It was the trial of his faith.

I think after forty years Moses had given up any idea of delivering his people, and it was only then that the Lord appeared to him. He appeared to him in the most extraordinary manner. I have always thought it would have been so wonderful if it had been one of those magnificent tall palm trees with that fire up there and the Lord saying to Moses: "Take your shoes from off your feet; the ground whereon you stand is holy." We who believe in Bible typology would have been thrilled with the palm tree, which would have signified holiness and righteousness; but the Lord did not appear in the palm tree. He did not appear in any of the other trees, not in an olive tree nor even in a vine. We who are charismatic would have been so thrilled if only it had been in an olive tree. No; He took the humblest, most insignificant, most worthless little bush in the desert, the thorn bush. They were found everywhere and were never higher than your waist. He did not even take a live thorn bush, which would have been something; He took a dead one. Then the Lord got into the thorn bush, and Moses looked down into the fire at the Lord and the Lord spoke up to him, saying, "Take your shoes from off your feet; this ground you stand upon is holy."

This was the trial of Moses' faith. I do not think he ever would have been able to respond but for those forty years. Now, the Lord was the I AM; now the Lord was going to be his strength, his grace, his power, his authority; the Lord was going to be everything he needed. The Lord was going to take this man back into Egypt and turn Egypt upside down and bring the whole might of the Egyptian royal family to zero—the first born dead—and then take out a nation of slaves through an impassable Red Sea.

David

There are many beautiful things about David. When David was a lad, Samuel came to his house. It had been revealed to Samuel that Saul was not God's king; and when he came to the family of Jesse, he went through all the great strapping boys, one after the other, and he said, "No." Jesse must have been so sad. Then Samuel said to him, "There must be someone else." Jesse had said that was all of them, but Samuel said, "There must be someone else." "Oh yes, there is the kid." Now I am not being funny, because when he carried the cheeses to his brothers when they were fighting Goliath, one of his brothers said to him, "Why are you so fresh, coming here? Do you want to see the battle?" They all looked upon David as the kid. It did not mean that he was tiny or weak or anemic; it just meant he was the kid. He was the last one in the family and probably divided by a few years from all the others.

Samuel said, "I want to see him." As soon as David came in, the Lord said, "This is he." And Samuel anointed him. When Samuel anointed him, it was a royal anointing. It was an unbelievable thing for Samuel to anoint him as king. Can you imagine the enemy coming to David and saying, "You are going to be king; watch out for the opportunity." The opportunities came. First, he got into the royal family with Saul. Then Saul got violently, demonically, maniacally jealous of him. He tried to kill him two or three times and David fled. Then we have two occasions when Saul was right in the hands of David, and you can almost hear the enemy saying to him: "Go on, David, this is your God-given opportunity. You are the one who is going to be king. Polish him off." David never did it, never. It was the trial of his faith. He was made king of Judah first in Hebron and then seven years later, king of Israel. It is a marvelous story. It was the trial of his faith.

Peter

You could say these are very great people; but in your circumstances, your situations, your conditions, the principle is the same. Actually, Peter is the greatest illustration of the trial of faith. In Luke 22 our Lord Jesus spoke these words: "Simon, Simon, behold, Satan asked to have you, that he might sift you as wheat: but I have [prayed] for thee, that thy faith fail not" (vv. 31–32).

I used to ponder on this. I heard so many messages on the failure of Peter's faith, the collapse of his faith, the denial of the Lord Jesus. When the Lord said, "I have prayed that your faith fail not," did it mean that the Lord was praying that he would not deny Him? No, not at all! The Lord was saying, "I am interceding for you, Peter, that that God-given faith that is deep within your heart—buried by pseudo faith, buried by counterfeit faith, with all its accretions and additions—given by My Father to you, will not fail in the hour of your shattering." And it never did. I know that this is not the ususal way of looking at Peter, but his faith never failed. Peter was shattered. The whole superstructure of his life as a disciple and as an apostle was blown to pieces by a spiritual, nuclear explosion. It wiped out every single thing on the surface. Peter was left with nothing, and he went out and cried. Judas cried, and he went out and committed suicide. Peter went out and cried, and he cried himself back to the Lord. His God-given faith never failed. All it took was one look from the Lord Jesus. When those eyes of the Lord Jesus met the eyes of Peter, suddenly, that God-given faith was renewed.

God Allows Satan to Sift Peter

There is something else in this marvelous story I want you to see, terrible as is it. Satan is the agent. What an extraordinary thing the Lord Jesus said. It is literally this: "Satan has obtained you by request." Satan cannot get you except by request. Think of that! If you are a child of God, Satan can never touch you unless he gets permission. Satan went to the Lord, to the Father and said, "I want Peter." The Father said to Satan, "You can have Peter." Maybe this is very strange to some of you, but God used Satan to sift Peter like wheat. God got the wheat; Satan got the chaff. That is what always happens. Every time we come to the trial of our faith, Satan gets the husks; God gets the fruit. The value, the treasure is reserved in heaven; Satan gets all that is worthless. I do not know why Satan does it, but he has been doing it for so many years. A proud person is a proud person. Being eaten up with pride must be the explanation. But every time he touches a child of God, God turns it to good account.

Peter's Self-Manufactured Faith

There is something else I want you to notice about Peter. We are dealing with what we can call a self-manufactured faith, a self-manufactured Christian life, a self-produced service. It is not that there is not something real in it, but somewhere along the line, we have taken over and produced a kind of Christian life, a kind of Christian service, a kind of church. On every level, it is the same. We do it. It may have all the Biblical facade; it may have all the outward trappings of something that is absolutely right, but it is self-produced, self-manufactured.

Peter had so much of the Lord; he had revelation. Nevertheless, he gets run down by people as being some kind of extrovert who was always opening his mouth and putting his foot in it. We almost laugh at Peter. But the Word says, "And so said all the others." Peter just happened to be the one of the twelve who was the spokesman. He said, often, what the others were too nervous to express, and therefore he got the trouble. There are many people like that. In a sense, he was in leadership; so he was the one who was always in the fire. He would jump in where angels fear to tread: "You are not going to the cross; certainly not! We are not going to let You, Lord. Of course not! We will be dead before You are dead; we are not going to let You go to the cross." But this was the same Peter who said, "Thou art the Messiah, the Son of the living God." This is the same Peter who said, "To whom can we go? You have the words of eternal life." He was a real servant of the Lord; he was a real apostle; he was a real child of God; he had a real relationship to the Lord. He had a real devotion, but a lot of it was mixed with that which had come from himself. It was a self-manufactured Christianity and service, and in the end, Satan was the one that God used to divide the pseudo from the real.

The Lord's Faithfulness Brings Us Through

It is the same with you. Don't fear when you come into situations which are terrible and dark. It may seem satanic to you, but God is dividing the pseudo from the real. Satan will get the chaff; God will get the wheat.

These words of the Lord Jesus are absolutely wonderful: "I have prayed for thee." Do you know that the Lord Jesus prays for you? Has it ever come home to you with living power and force that He actually prays for you by name? In II Timothy it says, "If we deny him, he will deny us; if we endure, we shall reign with Him; if we are faithless ..." Now we expect Him to say that He will renounce us, but it says, "If we are faithless, he remains faithful; for he cannot deny himself." If we come, finally, to the throne of God and to that place in our inheritance incorruptible, unsoiled, unfading, we shall come not because of our faithfulness but because of His faithfulness. In every believer's life, there comes a time when our faith collapses and we cannot even believe; then the Lord takes us through.

"Who shall lay anything to the charge of God's elect? It is God that justifieth; who is he that condemneth? It is Christ Jesus that died, yea rather, that was raised from the dead, who is at the right hand of God, who also maketh intercession for us. Who shall separate us from the love of Christ? shall tribulation, or anguish, or persecution, or famine, or nakedness, or peril, or sword? Nay, in all these things we are more than conquerors through him that loved us" (Romans 8:33–35, 37).

I Will Raise Him Up

When I was much younger than I now am, eighteen or nineteen, and in Egypt, there was a certain brother who was a very blessed, dear servant of God; but I did not agree with him at all.

He had a whole lot of views which I did not agree with, and I was outspoken and not afraid to say just what I thought. All the boys from the Air Force and the Army who were believers used to have great discussions in the Egypt General Missions house. I remember a discussion we had on election and predestination. I had an autograph book in those days, and I used to give it around to different people to put their autograph in. I gave it to this missionary, who was old enough to be my father. He wrote in it these words: "All that which the Father giveth me shall come unto me; and him that cometh to me I will in no wise cast out. And this is the will of him that sent me, that of all that which he hath given me I should lose nothing, but should raise it up at the last day" (John 6:37, 39). I thought to myself, "That is his predestinationalism;" but it is the Word of God. Over the years, I have thought and thought. I have never had any huge, cataclysmic experience; but I have come, finally, to see that in the mystery of God, and I will never understand it, there is a thing we call election. Everyone that the Father has given the Son will come to Him, and of those, the Son will lose not one. Why does it say, "And I will raise him up on the last day"? What a funny thing to add to it. Why doesn't the Lord say, "And I will not lose them and they shall be like Me"? or "They shall be with Me"? But he said, "And I will raise him up." It is because your body is the last part of God's salvation. Your body is going to be redeemed—a new body, a resurrection body. That is the last part of this so great salvation. Not a single thing will He leave to Satan. He has redeemed you— spirit, soul, and body—and at the end, He will have you.

Dear child of God, believe it. Maybe in your heart will be born a new faith that is alive, that works, that you may know you have a Savior that will not let you go. You have been given to Him by the Father. He will not let you go. He prays for you. He watches over you. Nothing happens to you by accident. Even when Satan is allowed to touch you, God uses it. This is the trial or proving of our faith, which is "more precious than gold which perishes though it be tried by fire, may be found unto praise and glory and honor at the revelation of Jesus Christ."

Shall we pray?

Dear Father, we pray for everyone who may be in such a proving of their faith that You will comfort and strengthen every such one. And for those who may not fully understand what is being said, we pray that you will keep it alive in our spirit and bring it into revelation at the time that we need it. Grant, Lord, that every one of us may know what it is to be guarded by Your power through faith unto that salvation ready to be revealed at the last time. Lord, may it be to praise, to glory, and to honor. We commit ourselves to You, Lord, because we are conscious that we are nothing and we are conscious how little we really love You when it comes to it. But one thing we do know, Lord, You love us and You have set Your love upon us and You have said, "All of those that the Father has given to Me shall come to Me, and I will lose not one of them." Lord, guard us and keep us and bring us to the fulfillment of all Your purpose for our lives. We ask it in the name of the Lord Jesus. Amen.

4.
Overcoming and Inheriting Faith

Hebrews 6:11–12

And we desire that each one of you may show the same diligence unto the [full assurance] of hope even to the end: that ye be not sluggish, but imitators of them who through faith and patience inherit the promises.

Hebrews 10:35–39

Cast not away therefore your [confidence], which hath great recompense of reward. For ye have need of patience, that, having done the will of God, ye may receive the promise. For yet a very little while, He that cometh shall come, and shall not tarry. But my righteous one shall live by faith: And if he shrink back, my soul hath no pleasure in him. But we are not of them that shrink back unto perdition; but of them that have faith unto the [gaining] of the soul.

James 1:2–4

Count it all joy, my brethren, when ye fall into manifold [trials]; knowing that the proving of your faith worketh patience. And let patience have its perfect work, that ye may be perfect and entire, lacking in nothing.

Hebrews 12:1–3

Therefore let us also, seeing we are compassed about with so great a cloud of witnesses, lay aside every weight, and the sin which doth so easily beset us, and let us run with patience the race that is set before us, looking unto Jesus the author and [finisher] of our faith, who for the joy that was set before him endured the cross, despising shame, and hath sat down at the right hand of the throne of God. For consider him that hath endured such gainsaying of sinners against himself, that ye wax not weary, fainting in your souls.

Shall we pray?

Beloved Lord, we want to thank You that we are here, gathered in Your presence. We thank You that You have made all the provision necessary for us to speak Your Word and to hear Your Word. Father, we pray that You will deliver us from merely the words of man or our own hearing. We want that Your Word shall come to us in a living, powerful way that we may meet with You through Your Word. To that end, Lord, we need our hearing touched by Your Holy Spirit. We thank You for that anointing grace and power that You have made available to us, and we stand by faith into it that the speaking, translating, and hearing all may be by Your power. Oh Lord, meet with us and deposit something within us and grant that we all shall be *men and women of living faith. We ask it in the name of our Messiah, the Lord Jesus. Amen.*

Finishing Faith

There is no more vital, strategic, necessary matter than living faith. We are living in days of artificiality and superficiality which is a very shallow kind of Christianity. It is a Christianity that is more on the surface—skin deep. Today we do not find the depth of character, sacrifice, or endurance that once characterized the church of God. This is very largely because we are not the possessors of a living, working faith. We are being influenced by the whole pagan society around us, with its pagan foundations and mentality. It is, basically, an anti-biblical society that we are now living in, and this is beginning to influence us greatly, so much so that we very often find within us an evil heart of unbelief. There are Christian cynics by the galore. They go to church, they take communion, they are baptized, they belong to churches. They even come among us and fellowship in assemblies of born-again believers, but just beneath the surface is cynicism: "Nothing works; we do not believe anything really works." We need a living, working faith that links us to the Person of the Lord and brings us into all the reality of what He has so dearly won for us at Calvary.

There is a faith that overcomes, a faith that inherits, a faith that perseveres and finally reaches God's goal. This is the kind of faith you and I need. Not only do we need faith that brings us into the salvation of God and faith that brings us into the realities that are ours in the Lord Jesus, but we need a finishing faith. As Margaret

Barber said in that marvelous hymn, we need the Lord to cast on us His Spirit so that we come right through to the end of the Lord, that we do not fall in the last part of the race, but we come right through to the end and obtain the prize.

Faith and Patience

"That ye be not sluggish, but imitators of them who through faith and patience inherit the promises" (Hebrews 6:12). It is not just through faith. It would be marvelous if every time we exercised faith, it immediately happened. It would be just like when the priests put their feet down into the swollen waters of the Jordan River, and immediately, the waters disappeared and they went over on dry ground. It is wonderful when the Lord answers faith like that; but there are other times when we have to go around the walls once a day for six days and seven times on the seventh day, and one wonders why. Does God have to get steam up? Is it, maybe, that He does not have the power? Of course not! I have no idea why. All I know is that the Lord could have brought down those walls of Jericho in one single moment, just like when He took them over the swollen Jordan River. But the Lord has His own way—faith and patience. They had to go around once a day, looking at those massive walls, watching all the armed Jericho people on the top, looking over. They were not allowed to talk. They were not allowed to discourage one another by saying, "These walls are never coming down. Look at their size; look at how massive they are." There was no talking. They walked in the heat of the day. Why wasn't the Lord merciful to let them walk in the middle of the night? Do you know that Jericho is the lowest place on the face of the earth? It is twelve hundred feet below sea level and four thousand feet below Jerusalem. It is unbelievable. It is always hot in Jericho. They grow mangoes and all the other tropical fruit there because it is so warm. Can you imagine those poor people having to walk around those walls once a day and then on the seventh day seven times? Faith and patience.

Faith always inherits, but the temptation is to cast away our confidence and faint in our souls. There is a prophecy in Isaiah which seems to me is being fulfilled in our day and generation and it says, "And the young men shall faint and be weary" (see Isaiah 40:30). It seems to me that many of the new generation come well within this category—fainting in their souls. What you and I need is not just initial faith, introductory faith, even developing faith; we need finishing faith, faith that will bring us to the end of the Lord, to the goal of the Lord.

James says, "Count it all joy, my brethren, when ye fall into manifold [trials]; knowing that the proving of your faith worketh patience. And let patience have its perfect work, that ye may be perfect [complete] and entire, lacking in nothing" (James 1:2-4). When the Lord tries our faith, it is to make it enduring faith or persevering faith. It is to tone up the muscle strength of our faith, as it were, to exercise it so that we will be able to endure steadfastly until we see the fulfillment of God's purpose and Word.

The End of Our Faith

Let us consider, first of all, the end of our faith. Why has the Lord saved us? I have never been able to understand Christians who believe that salvation is the end of the Lord. That is one of the most extraordinary ideas amongst Christians. Why do Christians think that salvation is the goal and objective of the Lord? It is perfectly clear when we look at the Bible that salvation is the means to an end, not an end in itself. In other words, by salvation, God has put us back in the race and on the course. God has constituted us in such a way that we can inherit by salvation; but we still have to inherit.

I believe this testimony of the apostle Paul in Philippians 3 is the most remarkable testimony in the Word of God, and he ended it in this way: "I press on toward the goal unto the prize of the high calling of God in Christ Jesus" (Philippians 3:14). The apostle was almost at the end of his life, on the threshold of his martyrdom, at the point where he was going to enter into the presence of the Lord; and here he was saying that in spite of his experiences, in spite of that heavenly vision, in spite of being caught up to the third heaven and seeing things not lawful to utter, in spite of all the revelations that had been given to him by the Holy Spirit, he was pressing on. He did not consider himself as having arrived, but he was pressing on toward the goal and the prize of the high calling of God in Christ Jesus.

Gaining Christ

In verse 8, he said, "I count all these things but refuse or dung that I may gain Christ." I want to suggest to you that this is extraordinary, unevangelical language. What did he mean: "That I may gain Christ"? Is not the Lord Jesus God's unspeakable gift to us? Do we not come into a union with Christ through the grace of God alone and not of works? Why then did he say, "I count everything to be loss"? He never despised his Jewish heritage.

He never despised his pedigree or his background, but he said, "I count the whole thing but refuse that I may gain Christ." He was saying, if it means I have that and don't gain Christ, then I will let the whole thing go.

What did he mean: "That I may gain Christ"? I would say to him, "Are you not saved?"

"Of course, I am saved."

"Are you not born again?"

"Yes, I am born again."

"Do you not know the Lord?"

"Yes, I do know the Lord."

"Then why do you say, 'That I may know him'?"

It is almost as if the more the apostle knew the Lord, the more he knew there was to know; as if the more he knew of the Lord, the more he knew how little he knew. He was inflamed with hunger. It is as if the more he had come to know the Lord and experienced the Lord, the more he realized he needed the Lord: "I need more of the Lord. What I have is so little compared to what is mine."

Laying Hold

What did he mean when he said, "Not that I have already obtained"? He said, "I lay hold on that for which I was laid hold on by Christ." What did he mean? He admitted that Christ had laid hold of him. He was a saved man, born of the Spirit, but he spoke of laying hold on that for which Christ laid hold on him. In other words, he has been saved to something. He has been saved to a goal, to a prize. He wanted to lay hold on that for which Christ laid hold on him. He did not count himself yet to have obtained.

Then I would say to him: "Paul, I want to have a talk with you. Have you written the Roman letter?"

"Yes."

"All of it?"

"All of it."

"Have you written the 1 Corinthian letter?"

"Yes"

 Have you written the 13th chapter?"

"Yes."

"Have you written the 15th chapter?"

"Yes."

"Have you written the 12th chapter?"

"Yes."

"Have you written all of the second letter to the Corinthian?"

"Yes, all of it."

So I would say, "The things that you say, the things that have been revealed to you, the things that you have experienced, I would think those things in themselves would be enough to get anyone into glory. What do you mean when you talk about forgetting the things that are behind and pressing forward? What has gotten into you, Paul? What has bitten you? Why do you have this insatiable hunger?"

The Prize of the High Calling of God

The way the Lord revealed it to me is very simple. Christ is given to us freely as Savior, but as Bridegroom, He is gained. All is of the grace of God, but it is what you do with the grace of God. All is by the power of God, but it is what you do with the power of God. He has given to us a Savior. We do nothing; we can do nothing;

we can only receive Him as Savior. But we have to press on toward the goal to the prize of the high calling of God in Christ Jesus. Where is the high calling of God? It is in Christ Jesus. The goal, the prize of the high calling of God is in Christ Jesus. How sad it is that most Christians' horizons are so small that they seem to think that all there is to the gospel is to be saved, to be forgiven, to be justified, to read one's Bible, to pray, to assemble, to gather with other believers and, if you are very zealous, to try and win others to the Lord. They think that is all there is, no more. There is a tremendous amount more.

I only know that the Holy Spirit is the only One who can open your eyes. It is not me speaking a lot of words that will do it; it is the Holy Spirit who will open your eyes. Suddenly, something opens within us in our spirit, and for the first time we see something with the eye of the heart. It changes us and spoils us for the rest of our lives. We can never be the same again. We have seen something. Our horizons, suddenly, have been extended, expanded; and we can never be happy again with small horizons. We are saved unto purpose.

A Race to be Won

We have the same idea in the race that the apostle Paul speaks of quite clearly in 1 Corinthians 9: "Know ye not that they that run in a race run all, but one receiveth the prize? Even so run; that ye may attain. And every man that striveth in the games exerciseth self-control in all things. Now they do it to receive a corruptible crown; but we an incorruptible. I therefore so run, as not uncertainly; so fight I, as not beating the air: but I buffet my body, and bring it into bondage: lest by any means, after that I have preached to others, I myself should be [a reject]" (vv. 27–29).

He is not a reject to salvation; he is a reject to the inheritance. He is not a reject in salvation; he is a reject to the whole question of reaching the throne of God. Now we suddenly discover that once we are saved, by the grace of God, we have started on a race, and there is a prize to be won in that race. We find ourselves on a course, in a race.

We find this also in Hebrews. All through the 11th chapter we have this great catalogue of faith, and then suddenly he says in chapter 12, "Let us run the race that is set before us, looking unto Jesus the author and finisher of our faith." He is the One who put us in the race and gave us faith to start the race; He is the One who will give us faith to complete the race and attain the prize.

Joint-Heirs with Christ

The Spirit himself beareth witness with our spirit, that we are children of God: and if children, then heirs; heirs of God, and joint-heirs with Christ; if so be that we suffer with him, that we may be also glorified with him (Romans 8:16–17).

It is the same thing all over again. We are told that the Holy Spirit has been shed abroad in our hearts, crying, "Abba, Father." It is a relationship to God. Then we discover that we are heirs of God, and joint-heirs with Christ. It is the Lord Jesus alone who is able and worthy to inherit, but the amazing thing is that by the grace of God we have been made heirs of God, and joint-heirs with the Lord Jesus. We do not deserve it; we are not worthy of it, but by His grace, He has made us His heirs and joint-heirs with His Son. And some people think the gospel is boring!

They think this whole thing of the Christian life is so boring. Of course, Christians have made it deadly dull. Because of the littleness of our vision and the littleness of our understanding, we have reduced this whole thing to a deadly boredom.

"Heirs of God." We do not even know what we are going to fully inherit. This poor, old, broken-down world is a disaster ecologically—polluted in air, in sea, in earth. This world, so marvelous in itself, is subjected to a cycle of corruption through sin and the fall of man. Like a Roman ruin, like a Greek ruin, we have just the faintest idea of what God originally intended this universe to be. But we are heirs of God and joint-heirs with Christ. We are being prepared to inherit. We have no idea what it will mean one day.

People ask me, "Will we have clothes?" How do I know? " Will we recognize each other?" How do I know? "Will we have pets?" How do I know? I cannot believe we will not recognize one another, unless the Lord thinks it might be wiser. People have said to me: "I had a lovely pet and it died. Will it be there in glory?" I say, "No, I do not think pets or animals have that kind of soul, but the Lord can create another." Christians have many questions, but if you know the Lord, you can trust Him.

We do not even know what the Lord ever intended in this old earth. All I know is that it is unbelievably beautiful, even in its ruined condition. Even in its pollution, in the destruction of so much of its ecological system, it is still incredibly beautiful. God has an enormous purpose which has been arrested, shelved, if you like, by the fall of man; but one of these days, all that belongs to the first things will have passed away and everything will be new. Then God will say, "Now we will get on with the job.

We will get on with what I first had in My heart." We do not even know what it is, but it is going to be so exciting.

People always want to go to the moon and these kinds of things. People have even booked tickets in the next millennium to go to the moon. Can you believe such stupidity! They will have to put on all that gear and sort of float around, not even being able to have a good meal. Can you imagine it! I do not want to go to the moon; but I do know that one day when the Lord comes, He is going to give us the kind of body that does not need all that gear, that does not need to sit in some great big contraption and be shot off from Cape Kennedy or wherever it is. We shall be in a universe without sin, in which righteousness dwells, and it will progress towards God's goal for the universe. The first thing is to bring us to the goal of our salvation.

No wonder the apostle Peter speaks about an inheritance incorruptible, undefiled, unfading, reserved in heaven for you, who by the power of God are kept through faith unto a salvation ready to be revealed in the last time. No wonder when he speaks about this inheritance, he speaks of the trial of your faith, the trying of your faith, the proving of your faith, the testing of your faith. It is worth it that you may be found unto praise, glory, and honor at the revelation of the Lord Jesus Christ. We have got an inheritance.

We are saved that we may inherit, just as the children of Israel were saved by the Passover lamb and delivered from the powers of darkness in Egypt and taken across into the wilderness. But that was not God's idea for them. He did not want them to live in the wilderness. His purpose for them was to inherit a land flowing with milk and honey. He wanted them to inherit that place where the house of the Lord would be built, where God would make known His name and manifest His power and glory. That was their inheritance.

The City of God

When we come to the last chapters of the Bible, we find a city. It is like no other city. I do not have any doubt that there will be a literal city one day where God and His people will dwell; I do not have any problem with this. But when people tell me that the city of God that is described in Revelation 21 and 22 is a literal city in the sense of the present city of Jerusalem, then I choke. How can you have a city that is so many miles broad, so many miles deep, so many miles high, and has only one street and twelve gates, and is transparent? Do you want to live in a city that is transparent from end to end? You can stand on one side and you can see everything that happens right through to the other side.

The Bride

Then again, this city is called a bride. Have you ever heard of such a thing? These two things are so different. A capital city speaks of government, of administration, of being the center of economics. A bride speaks of love, of union, of communion, of intimacy, of secrets shared, of a life shared. This city at the end of the Bible is the new Jerusalem; it is the wife of the Lamb.

Then we discover that this city is made out of three materials— gold, precious stone, pearl. All three of them speak of the character and nature of the Lord Jesus. It is as if the Holy Spirit is saying,

"Do you want to be in the city? Do you want to be part of the bride? Then you have to have gold." That is why Jesus said, "I counsel thee to buy of me gold refined by fire" (Revelation 3:18). You must have precious stone and pearl in your life. This city has no other materials. This bride, this wife of the Lamb is produced out of the character of the Lord Jesus, out of the life of the Lord Jesus, out of the nature of the Lord Jesus in sinners saved by grace. I find that quite amazing.

The Overcomers

There is a very beautiful little word that has been haunting me the last few weeks. I feel that I should just mention it because it comes into this. It is the way this whole vision ends.

"And there shall be no curse any more: and the throne of God and of the Lamb shall be therein: and his [bondslaves] shall serve him; and they shall see his face; and his name shall be [in] their foreheads. And there shall be night no more; and they need no light of lamp, neither light of sun; for the Lord God shall give them light: and they shall reign for ever and ever" (Revelation 22:3–5).

This is a very beautiful picture. Brother Sparks used to say that these are bondslaves. Not every Christian is a bondslave. These are the overcomers, and they are bondslaves. They do not consider anything as belonging to them. They believe they are the Lord's possession; they shall see His face. Our brother Sparks used to say that they shall be so near to the Lord that they can see His face. His name is in their foreheads. What does it mean? Just as the mark of the beast will be in the foreheads of those who do not belong to the Lamb, these have become so identified with the Lord Jesus that His name is engraved indelibly in their foreheads.

The great need is persevering, overcoming faith. If you and I are going to reach that throne and become part of that bride, if you and I are going to inherit our inheritance, if we are going to reign with Christ, then we need to be the possessors of an overcoming, inheriting faith. Such faith will bring us to a fulfilled salvation, a realized salvation. It will join us to the Lord. It will identify us with the Lord in such a way that we become not only followers of the Lamb but Lamb-like. Such faith will spoil us for anything less than God's goal. It is amazing how many Christians have prepared to settle for something far less than God's end. But once we have seen like Abraham—once the God of glory has appeared to us and we see His purpose in Christ, we see the city of glory in God, we are spoiled for anything less.

The Grace and Power of God

"Now unto him that is able to guard you from stumbling, and to set you before the presence of his glory without blemish in exceeding joy" (Jude 24).

Before I return to this matter of overcoming, inheriting faith, I want to explore this whole matter of the grace and power of God. "Him who is able to set you before the presence of his glory without blemish in exceeding joy." Get it! Wake up! Most Christians moan and groan. They have such problems, such circumstances, such situations. They have such difficult wives, difficult husbands, difficult children, difficult parents, difficult relatives. All of these things apparently rule them out, disqualify them from ever reaching the throne of God. God made a mistake when He saved you. Apparently, He had no idea about your circumstances and situations, about those difficult relatives of yours, and He saved you without regard to it. "Now unto him that is able to set you before the presence of his glory without blemish in exceeding joy." There are no regrets, only exceeding joy.

Did God go to all this trouble to save us and to bring us to this end of His and He does not expect us to reach it? I used to think, when I was first saved: Why did the Lord bother with us? It would have been much easier when Adam and Eve failed if He had said, "That's it! We will have a nuclear explosion and you are out. Now We will start again." He could have done it five or six times. Every time they failed they were out, and He would start again, until he got an Adam who did not fail. Wouldn't it have saved the Lord a lot of trouble?

We are all problems to the Lord. I feel so sorry, sometimes, for the Lord. I just know what He puts up with me; then I think of you. What a trouble we are to the Lord. When He saved us, we argued with Him. In the first flush of salvation, we coast along because we believe that the Lord is going to mollycoddle us and do lovely things to us; but as soon as He starts to refine us, as soon as He starts to purify us, we have the first argument with the Lord. We have the first rebellion. The first murmuring comes. We all are so difficult, even those sweet-faced people who seem to be so noble from the moment they are born. They become like dragons when the Lord really starts to deal with them. Why did the Lord bother with us? Why didn't He just wipe out Adam and Eve and start again, and if they failed, wipe them out? I do not know. If I had been the Lord, I would have wiped out Adam and

Eve. I would have started all over again, but the Lord did not. We only see in part; but it seems to me that the Lord realized, in the end, He would have something far more beautiful, something far more precious when He perseveres with these difficult, stiff-necked, problematic children of His.

Mildred Cable, an extraordinary missionary, whom I had the privilege of knowing when I was first saved, wrote a little book called "Parable of Jade". My great-uncle had quite a collection of jade before the Communists took it all from him, and it gave me a great interest in jade. Mildred Cable used to stay in my aunt's (not my real aunt—she adopted me as a believer) home, and I remember one day she spoke about jade in the fellowship. She told us that when the jade smith gets a piece of very beautiful jade, he wraps it in cloth, and he does not always do something with it right away. He will unwrap it, look at it, wrap it back up, and put it on the shelf. If it has a flaw or a fault he tries to imagine what he could do with it. She said that in some of the most precious pieces of jade, the fault has become the central point of the whole work. A little brown spot has become a bee on a flower, or a little black piece in a beautiful piece of pink jade has become a bird.

So it is with the Lord. He looked at mankind, and in some way, He knew that He was going to re-create us through our Lord Jesus. The most amazing thing is that, sometimes, He takes our very weaknesses and makes those the strongest point in His work in our lives. God expects us to reach His end. Let it get into your heart. In His eyes it is perfectly normal and natural for a born-again believer to reach the end of the Lord. He expects you to reach His end.

His life, His power and His grace will carry us right through every tribulation, every affliction, every difficult circumstance, and every condition of any kind until, finally, He brings us to His throne. It is like those birds that fly thousands of miles from north to south. They do not have a lesson before they go as to where they are going. They do not have a kind of bird Automobile Association that puts sign posts on the way. There is something inside, a life inside that tells them they have to go on and on and on. Sometimes, in Israel when I see the swallows come every spring and dive around our home, I think how amazing it is that they have come all the way from South Africa, thou-sands of miles south of us. They have come right up the whole continent of Africa, right across the desert to our area, and they are on their way to Moscow and St. Petersburg and Helsinki and Stockholm. What is it in them? These are fragile little birds that are so graceful. How do they do it? What tells them inside that they have some kind of swallow life that will not rest until it takes them right the way back to where they were born? If you are a child of God and the Lord Jesus lives within you, you have a life that originates in heaven. You have been born of God and that life and power and grace that has come into you will not rest until it has taken you back to the throne of God.

I always think one of the most wonderful, comforting, strengthening things about Pentecost is that when the Lord Jesus, who is at the right hand of the Father, took the Holy Spirit and poured Him out. It was as if He were saying, "This dear One, the Holy Spirit, God the Spirit, who was poured out as the promise of the Father, when He comes into you, on you, will enable you and empower you to go through every tribulation, every difficulty, until finally, you are back at the throne of God."

Christ in You

"The riches of the glory of this mystery among the Gentiles, which is Christ in you, the hope of glory" (Colossians 1:27). It is Christ in you. By the Holy Spirit, it is Christ dwelling in you. That is the hope of glory. It would be quite unnatural and abnormal if the Holy Spirit is in a person and he does not reach the throne of God. Wouldn't that be unnatural or abnormal if the Holy Spirit is really in you? Everything that has been created was created by the agency of the Spirit of God. When our Lord Jesus was born, it was the Spirit of the Lord that came upon Mary. When the church was born, it was the Holy Spirit that came. The Holy Spirit is in you. Don't you think that it is unnatural or abnormal to even consider that if the Holy Spirit is in you and on you, you will not reach God's end? It must mean only one thing, and that is all the power of God is available to you, all the grace of God is available to you to bring you to God's end.

Predestined According to Purpose

"And we know that to them that love God all things work together for good, even to them that are called ac-cording to his purpose. For whom he foreknew, he also foreordained to be conformed to the image of his Son, that he might be the firstborn among many brethren: and whom he foreordained, them he also called: and whom he called, them he also justified: and whom he justified, them he also glorified" (Romans 8:28–30).

It is almost as if the Spirit of God takes it all as accomplished. DONE! DONE! DONE! What are the troubles in your life? What are the circumstances? What are the difficulties? What are the problems? What are the satanic devices in your life? Where do the powers of darkness touch you? God will turn it, like with Job, all to good account. Because you are called according to purpose, He will use everything, even Satan himself, to complete you, to perfect you, to bring you to full maturity, to bring you to His throne. It is so wonderful.

Even if you do not share my view of predestination, you must surely accept this: "Those whom he foreknew, he foreordained." You have to accept that because it is in the Word. I am sorry they said "foreordained;" "predestined" is the old word. "Those whom he foreknew, he also predestined." What did He predestine them to? He predestined them to be conformed to the image of His Son, to be changed into the likeness of the Lord Jesus. That is all the predestinating power and grace of God behind the believer.

Are you saved? Are you a child of God? Have you been born of His Spirit? All the predestinating grace and power of God is behind you to bring you from a sinner to a saint, to change you from ugliness into the beauty of the Lord Jesus. As far as God is concerned, it is all done. "Whom he foreknew, them he foreordained, and whom he foreordained, them he called: whom he called, them he justified: and whom he justified, them he glorified." You have reached the throne; you have reached the city of glory; you have reached the Lord Jesus.

There are a number of Scriptures that tell us this: "The God of all grace, who called you unto his eternal glory in Christ" (I Peter 5:10a).

"Faithful is he that calleth you, who will also do it" (1 Thessalonians 5:24). It is over your whole spirit, soul, and body being preserved entire at the coming of the Lord Jesus.

"Being confident of this very thing, that he who began a good work in you will perfect it until the day of Jesus Christ" (Philippians 1:6).

Saved to the Uttermost

"Wherefore also he is able to save to the uttermost them that draw near unto God through him, seeing he ever liveth to make intercession for them" (Hebrews 7:25).

In other words, it is not just salvation; but once you are saved, He can save you to the uttermost—the throne of God, the bride of the Lamb—because He lives to intercede for you. Are we not extraordinary people? Most of us are not really honest when it comes to Christian things because we would never come out in the open with what we really think. But if we were honest, we would say, "I do not think most of us will reach the throne. I do not mean that we will lose our salvation, but when it comes to the throne, there will be only a very, very few. It is a rare thing, almost unique." What more can God do? He has put at your disposal all His power and all His grace to bring you to His end.

I have to travel a lot, so I am a "frequent traveler" on some airlines. The first time I flew on one of those jumbo 747 jets, I was sitting toward the front of the aircraft, watching everybody come in with all their hand luggage. Now I am not the least bit scientific, so I sat there thinking: "This thing is never going to get off the ground. Maybe I should get out of it while I can." I had never been in anything so big as that jumbo jet. As I sat looking out the window, it was like being on the second floor. As I watched all those people coming in with their luggage, I was thinking that if they all had luggage as heavy as mine and it is all stowed in this aircraft, this thing will never get off the ground. There is one thing I do know from experience, and that is the law of gravity. So I am always amazed when that great aircraft, filled to capacity with people, takes off from the ground because a superior power has taken over. There is a greater power than the law of gravity that lifts that great jumbo jet from the ground so slowly.

This is what I am trying to say. Just as that aircraft, with all its weights, all its hindrances, and everything that would hold it back is taken over by a superior power and it rises above those things until it is in the sunshine above the clouds, so it is with you and with me. God has not left us to our problems, to our besetting sins, to the weights that hold us down. He has given us life, He has given us power, He has given us grace; and that grace and power are superior to anything that could hold us back, if we will only believe.

Living, working faith is the thing that unites you to God. If you say, "I will never make it, I will never make it," you won't. If you think you are being humble before the Lord by saying, "I will never make it, I am too unworthy, I will never make it," you won't. Of course, we are unworthy; we know that. The Lord knows better than anybody just how unworthy we are, but He has made provision. When you trust in Him, something happens.

If you do not reach the throne of God, if you are not part of the bride, if you do not inherit your inheritance at the end, it is entirely your fault. Let me say it again: It is entirely your fault if you do not come to the end of the Lord. We all are so adept at blaming circumstances, blaming people, blaming conditions. We say, "I have never reached there because of so and so." The Lord says, "Nonsense; I made special grace available to you for that difficult person that you are living with. You never took it."

"Oh, but I am so weak."

The Lord says, "Nonsense! I made power available to you in your weakness so that you might come to My end."

You do not reach the throne of God through works; you reach the throne of God through grace. It is what you do with the grace. It is faith that takes hold of it; faith like a grain of mustard seed can take hold of the grace of God and the power of God and say, "It shall be done in my life!"

Have you ever said it in your family? in your domestic conditions? over your own personal life? over your own personal circumstances? over the ministry that God has given you? "It shall be done by the grace of God." You say, "That is presumption." No, it is not; it is the expression of faith. Once you know how unworthy you are, once you know how hopeless you are, once you know how problematic you are, once you know your tendency to let go or to faint in your soul, then it requires faith to say over yourself, "It shall be done! The will of God will be done in my life." Say it to yourself; let there be a confession of faith; let there be the word of your testimony. Learn to declare over yourself, your family, your business, your work life, the will of God.

Jesus, we are told, is the finisher of our faith. Why does it say that? In most Christian circles, it would suffice to say He is the author of faith. Why is He the finisher of our faith, unless there is a race to be run? He sets us on it, He produces and gifts us with faith, but we need finishing faith to come to the prize.

Problems with Living, Working Faith

Revelation

Some people say to me, "What is wrong with me? Why is there so little evidence of living, working faith in me and in others?" I can give you a number of reasons. The first is you are not looking to Jesus. There can be no faith without seeing the Lord with the eyes of the heart. Revelation is the key to everything. If we do not see the Lord Jesus with the eyes of our heart, there can never be a living, working faith. As we see Jesus, as we look to Him—not to a teaching, not to a system of teaching, not to a movement, not to an institution, not to other believers—then we discover living faith and finishing faith born in our hearts.

All hell conspired to keep Jesus in the grave, but He broke the power of Satan and all the forces of darkness and triumphed over them. Other people have been raised from the dead, but God raised them. Jesus laid down His life and took it again. It is marvelous. This same Jesus is in you. Are you telling me that there are circumstances that He cannot bring you through? He cannot break? He cannot solve? He cannot touch? Look to Jesus no matter what your condition, what your circumstances, what your situation. He has the keys of death and hell. There is not a key that will unlock something for you that He does not have; or if there is need in your life of something to be locked up, He has the key. You must see Him.

Fainting in Our Souls

Here is the second thing: We faint in our souls. When a person faints, they faint. They are perfectly normal one moment, and then all of a sudden, they are gone, collapsed, in a heap, fallen out, finished. They cannot do any more. We all have experienced something like that. We are going along so well, then suddenly, some situation develops and the enemy has come in. Oh, how clever the enemy is! He always produces a situation that gets under our skin and knocks us out, and we faint in our souls. I have known people who had been exercising faith and going along so well. They were growing in the Lord, and then suddenly, they fainted. Sometimes it was a very small thing, but for them it was a very big thing. It knocked them clean out.

Casting Away Our Confidence

Another thing is, we cast away our confidence. We had real trust, and then suddenly, we just threw it away. It is amazing that Christians do this. We have real confidence in the Lord; we are seeing the Lord; He is really with us, working with us and giving us grace to overcome and come out on top. Then all of a sudden, something happens and it is just too much for us, and we throw away our confidence.

Being Sluggish

Then there is another thing: We are sluggish. I think this word sluggish is a wonderful word. There are so many slugs among the brethren. It really is not a nice word, but it is a very descriptive word. Have you ever seen a slug? It moves so slowly. Some of us once ran, but now we are slugs. We are not even walking; our movement is minimal.

The Word of God says, "Don't be sluggish, but through faith and patience inherit the promises."

Fashioned According to This World

There is another reason: "Fashioned according to this world" (Romans 12:2a). One of our greatest problems with living faith is that we are fashioned according to this world. The only way we can get out of this trap is by the renewing of our mind; otherwise, we are fashioned according to this world. What does that mean? It is the wonderful thing that we hear about everywhere we go. When I was young in the Lord, I heard about it morning, noon, and night—Christian common sense. I was told that God has given you common sense; use it. But I had to say that the church was in a total mess through using this common sense. It did not seem to work. Nevertheless, they were always telling us to use our common sense.

In my experience, common sense is very rare. I would have said common sense is this: The Lord is here; the Lord has saved me and has saved me to a purpose. If the Lord has saved me with an end in view, He has surely made provision for me to reach that end. That is common sense to me. I would have said that common sense is trusting Him. Do you mean to tell me that He has persevered with mankind all these thousands of years, He has sent His Son to be the Savior of the world, He has taken hold of a little bit of human debris like me and saved me by His grace, and then thrown me out to the wolves? That is our common sense. Common sense tells me that if He has gone to all this trouble to make provision for me, I must stand in and appropriate that provision so that I come to His end. That is common sense, but it is very rare.

Most common sense goes like this: Do not be too spiritual. There is no point in being too spiritual; we are all human beings. Now I am not talking about those glassy-eyed mystics that we all know who cannot cook a meal, scrub a floor, bring up a child, or even keep a pet dog. They are the kind who go through life in a kind of daze; they are mystics. Everyone has to rush around and help them because they are fainting all the time. We think they are like Mary who sat at the feet of Jesus, as if Mary sat there with a glazed look in her eyes. It is so ridiculous. Mary was just as good at cooking as Martha, but she chose to be at the feet of Jesus. That is why Jesus said she had chosen the better part. We have got this idea of a kind of spirituality which means you are of no earthly use. This is not spirituality; it is religion. The real thing is that you have your feet on the earth, but you are not governed according to this world. Your concepts are not the world's. You know the Lord, you belong to the Lord, and you are part of a new man. You are His and He has given you all the grace and power.

Being fashioned according to this world gets us into so much trouble. It is why Abraham went down into Egypt. He had worked it out in his head: "Well, there is food down there, and there is no food up here." He used his common sense to go down to Egypt, and he got into a whole lot of trouble there. That is how Ishamel got born—because it was common sense. Sarah had an awful lot of common sense and she communicated it very well to Abraham and it stirred up his common sense. Together, their common sense produced one of the greatest disasters of human history. Being fashioned according to this world—this is the thing that destroys living faith.

Having an Evil Heart of Unbelief

Lastly, there is an evil heart of unbelief. It is interesting that the word calls it evil in a believer. Under the surface, under all the profession, under all the outward facade, there is an evil heart of unbelief. You need only a grain of living faith, and this grain of living faith will join you to the predestinating power and grace of God. It is irreversible, invincible, insuperable, all powerful. This living faith like a grain of seed of mustard seed can link you to the power and grace of God so that you come to the end of the Lord.

The Key to Overcoming

The Blood of the Lamb

In the book of Revelation, we have a very simple key given to us for overcoming: "They overcame [Satan] because of the blood of the Lamb, and because of the word of their testimony; and they loved not their life even unto death" (Revelation 12:11).

That requires faith. You can only overcome Satan if you know the finished work of the Lord Jesus, if you know all that that blood signifies. There is no other way to meet the accusations of Satan, no other way to meet the condemnation of the powers of darkness, no other way to meet your own unworthiness and unprofitability, no other way to meet your feeling of total inability but by the blood of the Lamb.

The Word of Their Testimony

It is more than that; it is the word of your testimony. This means that with your lips you say the same thing as God. You express with your lips the truth. This is not a testimony: "I think I am saved. I think;

I hope; I am not sure, but I am hoping against hope that one day I will be saved." This is not a testimony: "I think somewhere above the blue sky God is reigning, sometimes." The word of your testimony is when you say, "By the grace of God, I am saved. By the grace of God, I have been joined to God in the Lord Jesus." When you say, "He reigns over all"—that is the word of your testimony. When you say, "He is at the right hand of God and He has been made Head over all things to the church"—that is the word of your testimony.

That is why singing is so important. It says, "Singing one to another psalms and hymns and spiritual songs," because very often, in our songs we are confessing something: "Jesus shall reign wherever the sun doth its successive journeys run." It is a confession. We are stating something; we are declaring something. So often song or melody, when it is out of the heart, is a confession; it is the word of our testimony. Satan hates it because it is living, working faith in action. We are actually saying, "The blood of the Lord has covered me." Do you see the blood? No. Do you feel the blood? No. Then why do you say, "The blood has covered me?" It is a confession of faith. It is true, actually; more true than any other circumstance in your life, and Satan knows it.

When a child of God says, "He has saved me, sinner that I am," Satan can do nothing. He knows you are a sinner, but he knows that you have been saved by God. That is why he is attacking you. When you confess it with your lips, he can do nothing. When you say, "By the grace of God alone, I shall come to the end of the Lord," there is something that makes Satan tremble. He knows very well, better than you that God's grace is behind you, available to you and with you. The power of God is behind you; it is available to you; it is with you to bring you to the end of the Lord. When you confess it with your lips, he does not know what to do. He can only pile trouble after trouble on you in the hope that you will cast away your confidence or faint in your soul.

They Loved Not Their Lives Even unto Death

"They loved not their lives even unto death." The biggest problem we have in living, working faith is self. When we want to preserve ourselves, we get into a lot of trouble. Abraham wanted to preserve himself; that is why he presented Sarah as his sister. When we want to save ourselves, preserve ourselves, we get into a lot of trouble; we compromise. That is why it is absolutely necessary to lay down our lives for His sake and the gospel's. When a life is laid down, it does not mean that that person is perfect; far from it. But it does mean that when Satan comes, he does not have the same ground. The life has been laid down.

This is living, working faith, and only the Lord can open our eyes that we see Him. I do not want you to end with your eyes on faith. I want you to end with this: When we see the Lord, then we do the impossible. Then we live the Christian life, which by its very nature is impossible. Then we are being changed into the likeness of the Lord. Even if we are not conscious of it, others see it. The nearer we get to the Lord, very often the more hopeless we feel, but others see something of the Lord in us. We need to see the Lord, and as we see Him faith will be activated in us—not just beginning faith, but finishing faith. May the Lord Jesus work in all our hearts in this way.

Shall we pray?

Heavenly Father, we just lift our hearts up to You. We are unworthy and unprofitable servants. Lord, and You know it better than we. You know that left to ourselves, we make a mess of things. We make a mess of our lives; we make a mess of other people's lives; we make a mess of the church; we make a mess of the work of God. Oh Father, we need to be delivered from ourselves. We need to see You in a new way. Open the eyes of our hearts by Your grace, through the work of your Holy Spirit. Help us, perhaps for some of us for the very first time, to express real faith over ourselves, over our families, over our work, over our fellowship. Lord, meet with us. We thank You that You have made available to us all that predestinating grace and power of Yours, that same power that brought into being this universe. You have made it available to us to bring us to Your end. Oh Lord, deliver us from all those things that paralyze living faith and grant, Lord, that we may know a faith even as a grain of mustard seed that will join us to Your power, join us to Your grace, join us to Yourself. Lord, hear us. We ask it in the name of our Lord Jesus. Amen.

Other books by Lance Lambert can be found on lancelambert.org

Other books by Lance Lambert

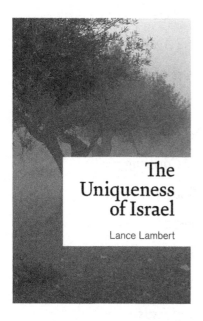

The Uniqueness of Israel

Woven into the fabric of Jewish existence there is an undeniable uniqueness. There is bitter controversy over the subject of Israel, but time itself will establish the truth about this nation's place in God's plan. For Lance Lambert, the Lord Jesus is the key that unlocks Jewish history He is the key not only to their fall, but also to their restoration. For in spite of the fact that they rejected Him, He has not rejected them.

Till the Day Dawns

"And we have the word of prophecy made more sure; whereunto ye do well that ye take heed, as unto a lamp shining in a dark place, until the day dawn, and the day-star arise in your hearts." (ii Peter 1:9).

The word of prophecy was not given that we might merely be comforted but that we would be prepared and made ready. Let us look into the Word of God together, searching out the prophecies, that the Day-Star arise in our hearts until the Day dawns.

Talks With Leaders

"O Timothy, guard that which is committed unto thee ..." (1 Timothy 6:20) Has God given you something? Has God deposited something in you? Is there something of Himself which He has given to you to contribute to the people of God? Guard it. Guard that vision which He has given you. Guard that understanding that He has so mercifully granted to you. Guard that experience which He has given that it does not evaporate or drain away or become a cause of pride. Guard that which the Lord has given to you by the Holy Spirit. In these heart-to-heart talks with leaders Lance Lambert covers such topics as the character of God's servants, the way to serve, the importance of anointing, and hearing God's voice. Let us consider together how to remain faithful with what has been entrusted to us.

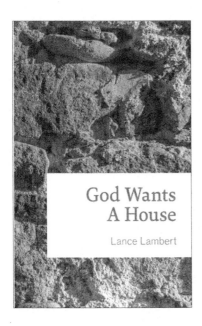

God Wants a House

Where is God at home? Is He at home in Richmond, VA? Is He at home in Washington? Is He at home in Richmond, Surrey? Is He at home in these other places? Where is God at home? There are thousands of living stones, many, many dear believers with real experience of the Lord, but where has the ark come home? Where are the staves being lengthened that God has finally come home? In God Wants a House Lance looks into this desire of the Lord, this desire He has to dwell with His people. What would this dwelling look like? Let's seek the Lord, that we can say with David, "One thing have I asked of Jehovah, that will I seek after: that I may dwell in the house of Jehovah all the days of my life, To behold the beauty of Jehovah, And to inquire in his temple."

Made in the USA
Middletown, DE
14 February 2024

49749133R00070